REVIVING OUR
INDIGENOUS
SOULS

How to Practice the Ancient to Bring in the New

Cathie G. Stivers

BALBOA
PRESS

A DIVISION OF HAY HOUSE

Scripture quotations are from New Revised Standard Version Bible, copyright © 1989 National Council of the Churches of Christ in the United States of America. Used by permission. All rights reserved.

Balboa Press books may be ordered through booksellers or by contacting:

Balboa Press
A Division of Hay House
1663 Liberty Drive
Bloomington, IN 47403
www.balboapress.com
1 (877) 407-4847

Because of the dynamic nature of the Internet, any web addresses or links contained in this book may have changed since publication and may no longer be valid. The views expressed in this work are solely those of the author and do not necessarily reflect the views of the publisher, and the publisher hereby disclaims any responsibility for them.

The author of this book does not dispense medical advice or prescribe the use of any technique as a form of treatment for physical, emotional, or medical problems without the advice of a physician, either directly or indirectly. The intent of the author is only to offer information of a general nature to help you in your quest for emotional and spiritual well-being. In the event you use any of the information in this book for yourself, which is your constitutional right, the author and the publisher assume no responsibility for your actions.

Any people depicted in stock imagery provided by Thinkstock are models, and such images are being used for illustrative purposes only. Certain stock imagery © Thinkstock.

Print information available on the last page.

ISBN: 978-1-5043-9445-1 (sc)
ISBN: 978-1-5043-9542-7 (e)

Library of Congress Control Number: 2018901820

Balboa Press rev. date: 08/28/2018

I dedicate this book to:

Source, for our very existence;
Mother Earth, for calling us Her children;
our ancestors, for their commitment to the continuation of life;
and my mother, for the igniting question
she posed to me many years ago:
"Where do you think God lives?"

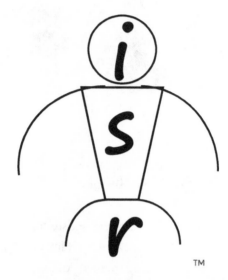

www.indigenoussoulrevival.com

CONTENTS

ACKNOWLEDGEMENTS

I am indebted to the following, for the contributions they made (wittingly or not) to the creation of this book. A deep bow of gratitude to you all:

Stephen Jenkinson and his Orphan Wisdom School, for cracking through my outermost and thickest layer of cultural ignorance and amnesia; for "wrecking me on schedule;" and for presenting me with a key to the etymology treasure chest.

Martin Prechtel, for the beauty you make in art and story; which stirred, fed, and re-membered *to* me and *with* me the Indigenous Soul in each of us.

Malidoma Patrice Somé, for your writings and your life purpose in action, modeling what it means to live in two worlds simultaneously.

Adam Rubel and Saq'Be'; and the Barrios Ajq'ij'ab (Carlos, Lina, and Denise) who collectively revealed to me, "There is nothing stopping you now."

The Wayfinders and the Woo-Finders (You know who you are!), and Myra Lovvorn, whose vision inspired the genesis and sustenance of both groups; and all the other Light Workers on the planet with whom I've rubbed spiritual elbows.

Jane Mitchell, my copy editor, for hearing my voice and facilitating its conversion to print form for a larger audience; and to her husband Tim, for asking me years ago, "When are you gonna write a book about this stuff?"

The fine people at Balboa Press, for their professional guidance and warm support during my first publishing experience.

Sylvia DeVoss, kindred spirit and alchemist artist, for the beauty you see and create, as exemplified in the book cover artwork.

Kristin Forburger, for your keen-eyed lens through which you see the world as a loving place, full of beautiful people, including the one you photographed for the back cover of this book.

My twin, Janet, for agreeing to come into this world with me, for reminding me who I am when I forget, and for modeling what is genuinely and simply true in this world.

My partner in life, Ann, for loving me unconditionally even when I am not so lovable; for supporting me on my journey even when it isn't easy to understand; and for constantly assuring me that who I am and what I offer is desperately needed in the world.

Preface

*Practices are the ways we hold the thread of story and weave through
or around the obstacles placed just where our attention must gather,
where genuine learning can occur.*

−Anonymous

When I was in kindergarten and my brother was in first grade, I discovered that while I was being read to, he was learning how to read. According to my mother, I hounded my brother daily until he taught me to read.

That insatiable desire to learn has driven me all my life.

In college, I majored in Health Science, because I wanted to learn as much as I could about this human body I occupy. I completed two graduate degrees in Public Health to teach young people what I had found so fascinating about being physically human. As a professor, learning even more about health, I became even more passionate about passing knowledge to my students.

This is who I am: a learner and a teacher.

Later in life, I immersed myself in spiritual studies, reading everything I could get my hands on about the spirit world and the infinite interpretations of it. Inevitably, I left my public health career to enter seminary. I longed to learn about the spiritual dimension within and surrounding us humans. Not knowing or caring what future occupation this learning experience would lead to, I predicted that the spirit realm for which I thirsted would guide me once I finished my formal studies.

I was right: upon completion of my Masters of Divinity degree, I became a chaplain and an ordained minister. Once again, I was ecstatic to be able to share what I learned and experienced, and I have been blessed with many varied opportunities to do so ever since.

This is who I am: a seeker and a minister.

While serving as chaplain in a pediatric long-term care facility, an email made its way to my inbox that publicized an event offered by Stephen Jenkinson (a.k.a. "Griefwalker"). I watched Jenkinson in the promotional video and instantly knew that I was to become a student of this amazing teacher. He was talking about life and death in ways that I had never heard before.

Enrolling in Jenkinson's Orphan Wisdom School launched me into ways of perceiving and understanding that were ancient, yet so new to me. I learned to consider what it means to be fully human, who and where I am in the universe, and how that universe operates.

My learning opportunities have increased exponentially since then. I now find myself at the most transcendent point of my lifetime of seeking, learning, and teaching. With heightened awareness, I have discovered that the "new" is just the "old" whose value has been rediscovered: What our generation calls a new age was dreamt into being by our ancestors.

Now, my models for learning are indigenous populations, those peoples who live in-sync with Mother Earth to honor her. My guides are shamans such as Martin Prechtel, Malidoma Patrice Somé, Carlos and Lina Barrios, and Joseph Rael. My teachers are fellow seekers like Carolyn Myss, Myra Lovvorn, and Steven Jenkinson. And my library includes ancient texts as well as new Earth/new age websites. Thanks to these multicultural spiritual influences, I have learned even more about who I am, where my place is in the universe, and what my life's purpose is.

As I was writing this book, a Maya shaman revealed to me what he saw as my purpose in this lifetime: to bring the past into the present in order to manifest the future. Happily, I was already embarking upon this very purpose—it is the intention of this book.

This book is my translation (literally a "carrying over, an offering, an extending") of what I've learned from other cultures into a form that is designed for those of us who grew up in the dominant, Western culture.

This is who I am: a translator and an author.

I wrote this book for the learner and seeker in me, so that I may use its guidance regularly for the rest of my life. I wrote this book for the teacher and minister in me so that I may teach and preach from it. And, I wrote this book to honor my life's calling and fulfill my life's purpose as a translator. I wrote this book because it is my destiny to do so.

I wrote this book for you, too, if you are:

- searching for the meaning of your life, and are open to what you might find;
- feeling a nudge or a strong calling toward something that you suspect might be your life's purpose or destiny, even though you may not be able to name it;
- sensing that this is an unprecedented time in planetary and cosmic history;
- courageous enough to think outside the box when it comes to understanding what it means to be human;
- willing to have your own beliefs and perceptions challenged, and perhaps even obliterated;
- intrigued by words like *new age, dimensions, chakras, consciousness,* and *ascension*; and
- hoping that you are not the only one entertaining these thoughts.

In this book, you will find practices for being fully human. To be fully human is to operate at capacity. But first we need to learn, or to remember, how great our capacity is.

Here's an analogy that might help: imagine you purchased a new computer. Right out of the box and charged, it's ready to perform innumerable functions. It is up to you to go beyond the basics, to explore and learn all the amazing things that it can do.

When we are born into this world, we're already constructed and wired adequately to perform at full human capacity. Being fully human means realizing and activating what we have been created to do. Critically, being fully human allows us to participate in cosmic shifts that are occurring now.

Why is this book different from the many other books on indigenous cultures or new age spirituality? A major difference is that I begin with the premise that as a human being, you are indigenous, no matter where your ancestors originate. This presupposition was introduced to me through the teachings of Maya shaman and teacher Martin Prechtel. This notion frees us to be genuinely indigenous without the risk of co-opting any particular practices of indigenous cultures. In other words, it means that I, a blonde-haired, blue-eyed woman of Western-European descent, don't have to be Native American to practice indigenous ways. Further, it means that I have a responsibility not to *try* to be Native American in order to act indigenously. The fact that every human being has an indigenous soul means that each of us has both the freedom and the responsibility of being genuinely who we are.

Another feature of this book is my intentional focus on linking past, present, and future together. I don't ask you to go back in time and live like our ancestors did; nor do I ask you to abandon the past in order to chart a future course. Instead, my teaching is based on the cosmic reality that past, present, and future are all happening at once, inextricably bound to each other.

Lastly but importantly, this book shares a methodology for delving deeper into ideas by using etymology, the study of words' origins and original meanings. Exploring the evolution of the key words in the title and chapter headings may help you broaden your understanding of the spiritual concepts and practices offered in these pages, and approach them differently as a result. This feature is described more thoroughly in Chapter 1, and by the time you reach the end of the book, you will have received lots of practice giving words their proper reverence. At times, I think you'll actually be amazed!

This book has asked quite a bit of me throughout the writing process, but it has rewarded me well for the work I've put into it. The same will be true of you as the reader: what you get out of this book will reflect how much of yourself you put into it.

To assist you, I offer some recommendations on how to use this book most effectively.

First, view this book less like a recipe book and more like an owner's manual. Although you will learn some how-to's and steps to follow, you will mostly learn about who you are.

Don't read more than one chapter at a time, in one sitting. Let it percolate. Or, read it straight through; and then go back and savor each chapter in its own right. Either way, read the book more than once or twice. It will teach you over and over again, if you're willing to read it multiple times, over time.

If a chapter or concept doesn't make sense or doesn't resonate with you the first time you read it, don't worry. Pass over it and come back to it another time. Often something that has little meaning to us at one point in time is packed full of meaning at a later time. When the student is ready, the teacher will come. When the reader is ready, the meaning will be there. And if it never shows up after multiple attempts over time, then that's okay, too. Don't feel like everything in these pages has to resonate with you. In fact, you may find much here to disagree with. That's fine, but make sure you've opened up to the possibility of its value to you before discounting it without trying it on.

Regardless of your proclaimed faith or religious/spiritual beliefs, you are encouraged to be open to how these chapters may enhance rather than threaten your current beliefs. This is especially true if you are willing to explore your faith tradition's mystical side, for it is in those esoteric meanings that you will find a great deal of consistency and compatibility with the practices offered in this book.

Consider that what you are reading is telling you something you already know, in your sub-conscious or super-conscious. This will require your attention and reverence for the interaction between the content and yourself, in order to discover how much you knew, but didn't know you knew! If you find yourself nodding your head while reading, or experiencing an "Aha!" moment, it means the words are speaking a language that some part of you knows.

Offered at the end of each chapter are opportunities to reflect on how the content applies to you, and some suggestions for putting into practice what you've just read about. In addition, I invite you to come up with your own methods of reflecting on the verbs and putting them into practice. Sometimes the best practice may be reflecting on it, praying about it, and letting it take seed in your inner garden. In this regard, the practices of meditation, contemplation, and journaling suit every chapter in this book.

The final chapter, "Coordinate," and the Appendix are designed to help you pull everything together that you've read throughout the book. Many of the chapters make reference to these closing sections of the book, and they direct you there accordingly. The explanations and visuals there are concise, and may require some pre-existing knowledge about or familiarity with the topics they cover. You are encouraged to do some additional research on your own to enhance your understanding and application of this information.

I recommend that you replace "practice makes perfect" with "practice makes action." Perfection is not the goal when practicing these verbs. The goal is to perform them in your life, in the infinite number of ways that you can.

Do more research on the words and concepts that you find in this book, including their etymologies. Similarly, look up the references cited throughout the book, and add them to your "for future reading" list. The value of this book is not only in the information it provides outright, but also in pointing you toward further exploration and self-initiated learning.

Finally, and most importantly, please don't embrace this book as a self-improvement tool. Instead, think of it as a self-realization or self-actualization tool. You were born whole and sufficient, you just need to realize it. You were born gifted and powerful, you just need to actualize it. Carry this book and refer to it as both a certificate of your authenticity and your marching orders. You are enough, so let this book help you remember that. You are called to go out and be enough, so let this book help you remember how.

1

WORD

Without knowing the force of words, it is impossible to know more.

–Confucius

I once had a dream about the force of words. It happened during my seminary years, as I was learning how to read, translate, and interpret Biblical Greek and Hebrew as part of my academic studies.

In my dream, I was doing my homework—reading an Old Testament passage in Hebrew and deciphering its meaning. With deep concentration, I stared at the lines of the text, and then suddenly the letters began to dance. They did their own version of the Rockettes performing at the Macy's Thanksgiving Day parade. At first I was in disbelief, and thought I was imagining things. But then I laughed out loud with glee as I thought, "My classmates will never believe this!"

"You're having fun?" the letters asked me.

"Oh, yes!" I giggled.

"Well, if you think *this* is amazing, come closer and look *behind* us. You'll *really* be blown away."

The dream ended before I got the full, behind-the-scenes view. But I was changed forever by the truth these dancing letters demonstrated: Words are alive.

More than a decade later, I was mentored by a teacher who encourages his students to look up the original root and meaning of a word—its etymology—in order to benefit from its history and full expression. His recommendation has become a cornerstone of my continuing education, and is credited for the format of this book.

Throughout the book, I used an online etymological dictionary[1] to identify the original root of a word, and roughly trace some of its history. The oldest written account of these roots dates back to the 4th millennium BC, or even earlier. This account is associated with "the prehistoric people of Eurasia who spoke Proto-Indo-European (PIE), the ancestor of the Indo-European languages according to linguistic reconstruction."[2] These ancient Eurasians are our ancestors, and their words resonate more or less in our 21st-century written and spoken languages. For some of the words explored in this book, little has changed in their meanings over thousands of years. For others, significant changes have occurred, revealing a gradual and detrimental stray from our indigenous beginnings.

The etymology of the key words in this book's title and chapter headings inspired and informed my writing process. Many a time when writer's block crept in, I followed my own advice and went back to the etymology for guidance.

That's what words are: guides. When we seek their help, they speak to us. In fact, the etymology of "word" indicates that the oldest known PIE root is *were-, which means "speak, say."

In this chapter, the key words in the book's title are examined, and their meanings interpreted. The same process is then performed on each chapter title, all of which are verbs. Surprisingly but not coincidentally, "verb" and "word" come from that same PIE root *were-. Thus, the importance of the origins of words includes the actions they convey.

Now let's look at the etymology of the key words in the title:

Revive – This key word is made up of re-, which means "again," and –vive, which comes from the PIE root *gwei-, meaning "to live." "To bring back to notice or fashion" is a meaning that came later. Together, these meanings indicate that reviving involves either bringing back to life something that was or appeared to be dead; or bringing back to our attention something that had been discarded or forgotten; or perhaps some of both.

Indigenous Soul – "Indigenous" literally means "in-born," so it points more toward something that was *born within* than it does to where something or someone was born. It comes from the PIE root *gene-* which means "give birth, beget." "Soul" comes from the Proto-Germanic *saiwalo* and Old English *sawol*, meaning "spiritual and emotional part of a person, the animate existence of life or living being."

Throughout his writings, Martin Prechtel refers to the "Indigenous Soul"[3] as the most ancient and most original part of everything and everyone, which remembers its true nature and lives it in coherence with all of creation. Those who are still called "indigenous people" today are the ones who have remained successful in honoring their indigenous souls, and have maintained their balanced lifestyle that is in sync with nature. Most of us in the 21st century have forgotten what it looks like and feels like to live indigenously. Nonetheless, this indigenous soul is in each one of us, stirring.

Practice – The earliest known roots for this word are the Greek words *praktos* ("done; to be done; to do, act, effect, or accomplish") and *praktikos* ("fit for action or business; practical; active, effective, vigorous"). Later definitions emphasize that practice is applied, not theoretical; and that it is performed repeatedly to improve skill. Practice involves repeating an action or performance, consistently working at or exercising it.

"Practice" is the most important word in the title, because it is the entire focus of the book. Accordingly, every chapter after this one has a verb as its title. All but one of these verbs are active, not passive, because ushering in the new age requires active participation, engagement, and movement. "Any time a human acts or moves,"

Joseph Rael tells us, "that movement is also a service to the cosmos, because of who we are."[4]

Being fully human requires action. The chapters and Appendix that follow offer thirty-one verbs (several are nouns that have been "verb-ed," translated into action) as guides on how to live fully human, especially during this time of unprecedented change.

You may be wondering, "How were these particular verbs selected, and what determined the order they're in?" At the risk of appearing random, these verbs just came to me, in one sitting, as I took pen to paper and listed what seemed to be obvious. Over time, few changes were made to the list, as the original verbs withstood the test of time and the evolution of the book. They are robust, and collectively capture the main actions that I perceive we humans are called on to perform in our lifetimes in order to live in sustainable and nurturing balance with Mother Earth and all her children.

Furthermore, these verbs/practices are interrelated (this cannot be over-emphasized!), sometimes giving the appearance of repetitiveness or redundancy. This is a feature of their inter-coherence and interdependence. The verbs affirm and point to each other, collectively forming a recommended path of practice. As such, the order of the chapters may give the false impression that there is a linear or chronological sequence in which to practice the verbs. While some practices necessarily build on others as a person ages and matures, most of these practices are appropriate for the age of puberty and beyond. They are also complementary—they call for us to not only perform these actions, but to also be grateful recipients when others practice them on behalf of the greater good.

Ancient – As an adjective, this word comes from the Vulgar Latin word, *anteanus*, literally meaning "from before." It is also related to *anti-* ("against; related to") and *ant-* ("front, forehead, facing opposite"). Derivative meanings include "in front of" and "before." Specifically in history, it means "belonging to the period before the fall of the Western Roman Empire," and is contrasted with *medieval* and *modern*.

In its noun form (as it appears in the title), "ancient" has a 1550s definition of "standard-bearer." This is believed to be a corruption of *ensign*, a 15th century word meaning "a token, sign, symbol; badge of office, mark or insignia of authority or rank; a low-ranking military person." *Ensign* comes from the Latin word *insignia* which means "badge of honor or office; mark, proof, sign, token." The *—sign* part of this word has additional meanings that deserve attention. *Sign* means, "to designate, distinguish, to make a mark upon." It is related to the root *sekw-*, which means, "to follow." This is also the root of *sequel* which means "that which follows or results, consequence; accompanies."

Based on the variety of meanings associated with this one word, "ancient" appears to link past, present, and future: It includes what has come before (past), what has marked us (past into present), what accompanies us (present), and what follows (present into future) as consequence (past, present, future all at once). The ancient practices prescribed in this book, then, are indeed timeless. They were fitting for our ancestors, they are fitting for us now, and they will be fitting as long as there is human existence.

Bring – This word comes from the root *bher*, meaning "to carry, to bear." The Old Norse word "barrow" (as in wheelbarrow) is related, and means, "I catch, I bring forth." Other meanings include "produce," "present," and "offer." Collectively, these meanings indicate that the new era is not an event that happens to us, but an event that needs us to carry it forward into existence. Every human being is invited to participate in the ushering in of the new world.

New – Original meanings of this word include "fresh," "recent," and "different from the old." According to prophecies from indigenous peoples and sacred writings in various world religions, Earth and humankind are on the cusp of a new era, a path leading to the return of a time of peace, equality, unconditional love, abundance, health and longevity. For thousands of years, earth-based cultures and seers of major religions have prophesied the planetary and galactic events that accompany this shift. Today, intrigued researchers from many disciplines (e.g., science, history, anthropology, theology) offer some legitimacy to these ancient claims.

The word "prophecy" is a combination of two root words. The *–phecy* part comes from the root *bha* which means "to speak." In particular, it means a reputation-based speaking. *Pro-* means "before," so "prophecy" means speaking with authority about something before it happens. Unlike a prediction, a prophecy isn't something that will automatically happen. What the prophet reveals is not absolute. Rather, the prophet speaks to the high likelihood of the event occurring if the warnings go unheeded. While the event itself cannot be altered or averted, it is possible to take appropriate actions to minimize the event's damage. Basically, a prophecy says, "Here's what's coming; here's what you can do to reduce its impact or to survive it intact."

The new era that the prophecies describe is a natural part of the 26,000-year cycle that follows a repeating pattern of changes in the movements of planets and other galactic bodies, as well as alternating periods of rises and falls in human consciousness and thus human culture. We have just exited a 13,000-year period of decline, and we are now taking our first footsteps into 13,000 years of shifting into higher consciousness, higher vibration, and greater awakening to our highest potential as human beings and to our connection with each other and our environment.

This new age (informed by and built upon earlier ages) is also referred to as the Age of Aquarius (astrology), the Kali Yuga (Hindu), and the Fifth Cycle or Fifth Sun (Maya). One of the Maya calendars ended on December 21st of 2012, identifying it as the end of the Fourth Cycle, and the beginning of the Fifth (called the Age of the Fifth Sun). Scientifically speaking, a galactic alignment occurred on that date, where the Winter Solstice sun lined up with the center of the Milky Way galaxy. This event takes place only once every 26,000 years.

The cyclic or patterned nature in these descriptions of the new age gives credence to the "fresh, recent, and different from the old" translations of "new." However, consider these additional etymological meanings of the word "new:" "unheard-of, untried, novel, and inexperienced." The spiritual evolution of Earth and her inhabitants is happening far more rapidly than has ever occurred at any time or place in the galaxy. Further, the unique feature of this particular time is that of ascension, which is "the attainment of spiritual knowledge, when we become primarily light rather than dense; a transformation from a focus on ego or personality to functioning from our Soul Self, love, and humility."[5]

The word "ascend" comes from the Latin *ascendere*, and is made up of two parts: *ad* ("to, toward"), and *scandere* ("to climb"). Its PIE root *skand-* means, "to spring, leap, climb." The upward movement that is starting to take place in this new era refers to the increase in energetic vibrations of Mother Earth and of humanity. Planetary ascension involves an increase in energetic vibrations in response to an influx of galactic energy that is reaching Earth's surface. Human ascension is also a result of the incoming galactic energy surges, and involves our navigation of the energetic relationships we have with every living thing (which is everything) all around us. Everything is simply energy, and one aspect of being fully human is how we manage our personal energies in relationship with the energies that surround us. Our indigenous nature understands these energetic influences, and provides the basis for acting accordingly, in balanced relationship with *all* living things. Being fully human in this new age will require us to realize that we are earthly and galactic humans simultaneously.

The Maya have long understood these energetic relationships. What contemporary culture calls quantum physics, the Maya have known about for thousands of years! Carlos Barrios, Shaman and Member of the Maya Elders Council, writes extensively of the ascension of Earth and humanity in his 2009 book, *The Book of Destiny: Unlocking the Secrets of the Ancient Mayans and the Prophecy of 2012.* Here is how Barrios describes this new age that we've just entered:

> "It will be a time of cleansing, when all of the garbage in our minds, all of our consumerism, will be cleared away and replaced with a resurgence of true spirituality and a renewed respect for ourselves and everyone else on this planet."[6]

> "Full consciousness will be activated in Mother Earth and humanity, hopefully generating a cycle of mental and spiritual growth, of true realization."[7]

> ". . . a time of harmony, peace, tolerance, and balance; ushering in a new framework that will modify the socioeconomic system."[8]

> ". . . enabling us to encompass the whole of the earth with our sight, and travel the universe in our thoughts and have the power to present ourselves to the Great Father, Heart of Sky."[9]

Revive. Indigenous Soul. Practice. Bring. Ancient and New. These words, and the verbs heading the following chapters, are a force. Without them, it would be impossible for us to know more about the meaning and purposes of our lives at such a time as this. If you're ready to learn what the words are saying to you, and the practices they ask of you, proceed to the next chapter.

2

BREATHE

Really, only one thing exists, and that is the breath of God in a state of movement creating the vibration of matter. Breath is the inspiration in matter that brings all concreteness or form into existence via movement.

–Joseph Rael

Breathing may seem so basic and so obvious that it doesn't really need elaboration. However, there are people for whom breathing is difficult. And, for those of us who breathe easily, there is a tendency to take this bodily function for granted. Doesn't our breathing deserve a few moments a day of our undivided and reverent attention?

"Breathe" comes from the word "breath," and the original root of "breath" is *gwhre*, which means "to breathe, smell." Everything starts with breath, as the opening quote indicates. This is especially true about human birth: fetus becomes human when it leaves the water environment of the womb and enters the environment of air.

What happens in that first breath? The word "smell" derives from a root meaning "hot," and is the precursor to "smolder," which means "burn and smoke without flame" and "exist in a suppressed state; burn inwardly." These words and phrases describe our condition during prenatal development—we *cook* into our fullest. The lungs are one of the last body parts to fully develop prenatally, and many a respiratory therapist in perinatal and pediatric intensive care units have stated about their tiny patients on ventilators, "They just have to *cook* a little more before they can breathe on their own."

Although not etymologically related, "inspire" comes from the Latin word *spirare*, "to breathe," and *spiritus*, "breath of life." To inspire means literally "to blow into, breathe upon;" and figuratively "to excite, inflame." Before birth, our essence smolders within us, awaiting air. Our first inhalation ignites us and launches us into humanity. Each inhale thereafter, as well as its exhale counterpart, fans our flames. "Respire" comes from the same Latin roots as "inspire." To "respirate" is to repeatedly breathe in and out, instinctively fanning our internal flames for the rest of our lives, until we expire, or breathe our last breath.

Breathing, then, is not only a physiological process. It is very much a spiritual one. From an indigenous standpoint, the two are not separate. Whenever we breathe in, we draw the spirit into us and are enlightened by it. Native American author and artist Jamie Sams writes:

> In the Native American culture, we are taught that
> the Spirits ride the wind. Wind, found in humans,
> is called the breath. When we breathe air into our
> bodies we are able to access the creative inspiration
> we need. Allowing Spirit to use the breath, to enter
> our physical forms, is illuminating.[10]

Each time we inhale, we are inspired, literally and figuratively. Each time we exhale, we release the spirit in a form that has been changed, influenced by its momentary contact with our unique internal flames. And that expired air now becomes available for the next person's inspiration. Repeatedly and perpetually, we create with our very breathing. When we inhale, we absorb the motion and thoughts of all around us whose exhalations we're breathing in. Multiply this process by the number of respirations each person performs daily, and then by the number of people on the planet, and it becomes mind-boggling how much inspiration is being circulated every day!

As everyone knows, breathing is physiologically an involuntary action, meaning we don't have to think about breathing for our respiration to continue. As a result, we often become lazy with our breathing, forgetting its miraculous process, and taking for granted its life-giving power.

Reflect

1. How often are you consciously aware of your breathing?
2. Have you ever thought of your own breath as spirit?
3. Have you ever saved someone's life with your own breathing? Has your life ever been saved by someone else's breathing?
4. Has it occurred to you that you are breathing the same air that others around you are breathing? What does it mean to you that we're all sharing the same air?

Practice

1. Learn good breathing techniques that will adequately saturate your body's tissues with the oxygen it needs. Here are some basic techniques for health-promoting breathing:
   - Inhale deeply through your nose, filling your abdomen with air.
   - Pause briefly, holding the air in your lungs.
   - Exhale through your mouth or nose. Push the last bit of air out of your lungs by contracting your abdominal muscles.
   - Pause briefly, before taking the next breath.
2. To incorporate the spiritual component, try one of a wide variety of practices prescribed by teachers of Eastern thought modalities, such as yoga, qigong, meditation, or body prayers.

3. Get into the practice of offering a whisper of your life-filled breath to the food you are about to eat, to the prayer you just prayed, to the morning you just greeted, to the car you just started, to the money you just received and to the bill you just paid, to the bed you retire in and the sleep state you will enter . . . and so on.

4. Breathe like your life depends on it, because of course it does. Breathe like you're pulling heaven into your body and then pushing it back out to share it. Breathe in a way that honors everything as living and breathing, exchanging life force with all. Breathe like that.

5. Celebrate your successful practice.

6. Repeat as needed.

3

BE FED

Let there be work, bread, water and salt for all.

–Nelson Mandela

Even though they both have a common goal of satiation, "eat" and "be fed" are not the same thing.

The PIE root of "eat" is *ed-. This is the source of "edible," which literally means, "I eat." Fast forward four or five thousand years to find the Old English derivative *etan*, which means "to consume food; devour." "Consume" comes from the Latin word *consumere*, which means, "to use up, eat, waste;" and is made up of the combination of com- ("with") + sumere ("to take"). "Devour" means "to swallow down; to accept eagerly." Both of these terms imply an assumed power or authority of the eater over the food, due to the eater's failure to recognize food as a life-giving substance upon which he relies for survival. To consume or devour food is to conquer and annihilate it, solely to achieve satiation.

In contrast, "feed" comes from the PIE root *pa- meaning "to tend, keep, pasture, protect, guard, feed." The Old English word *fedan* means "nourish, give food to, sustain, foster." To be fed is to be in a giving-receiving relationship with food, one that honors both parties fully and equally. To be fed is to be aware of how dependent we are upon food, not just to fill us, but to nurture us. When we contemplate that other living things die in order to feed us, then gratitude becomes another feature that distinguishes being fed from eating.

Martin Prechtel describes "five layers of initiation into becoming a Magnificent Adult:"[11]

1. birth to adolescence
2. adolescence to child-rearing
3. child-rearing to grandchild-rearing
4. grandchild-rearing to adult/elder
5. adult/elder to death.

These layers are not inconsistent with our Western models of human development, yet their focus is primarily on one's role in the village as opposed to one's individual achievement or progress. From an indigenous perspective, peoples' relationship with food changes according to what layer they are in. At birth and through the infant years, babies are fed as a matter of survival. Gradually young children enter into relationships with food as they learn where food comes from, who provides it, and other such connections. As children approach their teen years, they gain an understanding that being fed is about more than surviving. They grow into the knowing of the nurturing and tending aspects of being fed. They learn from the adults in their lives their culture's facts, ideas, beliefs, and behaviors about food. In short, they develop a relationship with food, and with all who feed them.

The progression from *be fed* to *feed* is a developmental one. *Being fed* is appropriate for young children until they reach puberty, the age where rituals of initiation into adulthood begin. In the second and higher layers, adults are called on to *feed* and finally in the fifth layer to *be the food* (addressed in future chapters).

We in the modern Western culture should have mastered the shift from *being fed* to *feeding* as young adults, but many of us have failed to do this. In general, the typical Westernized adult neither knows where his food comes from geographically, nor when certain foods are in season. He neither examines the environmental repercussions of his food choices, nor gives a thought to the fact that in order for him to eat, something had to die. The typical Westernized adult is a consumer—he *eats*.

To the indigenous soul, where and how food is grown, harvested, hunted, or gathered is meaningful; honoring the lives sacrificed to feed us is essential; and the relationship between humans and food is sacred. In reviving our indigenous souls in the 21ˢᵗ century, we must recover and restore this relationship. How do we accomplish this? In this culture at this time, we have all the information and resources we need. What we lack is a sense of honor.

Reflect

1. How would you describe your relationship with food?
2. What is the origin (i.e., the living being it came from) of the foods that comprised the meals you ate today?
3. Considering the difference between *eat* and *being fed*, which do you do when you partake of food?
4. When someone serves food to you, how do you feel? When you serve food to others, how do you feel?
5. How does food influence your relationships with other living beings in your life? (humans, animals, plants, etc.)

Practice

1. Honor yourself with nutritious food that is good for you—food that is whole, minimally refined and processed, non-genetically modified, and naturally grown.
2. Seek access to such food, regardless of your income, location, race, or societal status. You are worthy of it.

3. Honor yourself with the reality that plants and animals are dying to feed us. Further, accept and embrace your worthiness of killing them in an honorable way, so that you may be fed.

4. Honor yourself with the intention of being fed. You are worthy of receiving nourishment.

5. Honor your food. It is worthy of living a healthy life and experiencing a painless death.

6. Honor your food with an understanding of its place in the ecosystem and a promise to maintain that ecosystem's health. It is worthy of being thanked for its role in the cycle of life and death, and its sacrifice to feed you.

7. Honor your food with a willingness to pay a higher price for the nourishment it provides.

8. Practice modesty regarding portion sizes despite an "all-you-can-eat" environment. Your food is worthy of non-gluttonous behavior.

9. Give your undivided, gratitude-soaked attention during mealtime. Remember that the relationship you have with your food needs to be tended, kept, guarded, and protected. It needs to *be fed*.

10. Celebrate your successful practice.

11. Repeat as needed.

4

INTER-DEPEND

To say my fate is not tied to your fate is like saying,
"Your end of the boat is sinking."

–Hugh Downs

When my sister and I were in college, a friend invited us to her family's farm to help make apple butter. She told us to bring some good bread, some empty jars with lids, and our stirring muscles. When we arrived in early morning we discovered that preparations for this annual event were well underway. A dozen or so women had gotten up before sunrise to peel and core several dozen bushels of apples. The men had set up a huge copper kettle over the fire pit and had stacked an enormous pile of firewood nearby to keep the fire going on into the afternoon. The apples and other ingredients had to cook for most of the day, and the aromatic concoction had to be stirred non-stop, to prevent the apple butter from sticking or burning on the bottom of the kettle. With the exception of small children and frail elders, everyone present took their turn at stirring.

When at last the apple butter was done cooking, the fire under the kettle was extinguished, and we all sat down for a huge meal together while the apple butter cooled enough to be handled. We then brought our jars over to the kettle area, where one by one they were filled with the steamy apple butter. As a final communal activity, we were invited to bring our bread kettle-side. There, we pinched off pieces of bread and mopped the remaining apple butter off the inside of the kettle, and ate as many bites as our already-full stomachs could hold.

By dusk, everyone was tired and too-well fed, and each family gathered their apple-butter bounty that would last them until next fall, and headed home. Driving back to our college dorm, my sister and I talked about how important and how wonderful community support and love are, and realized that this is how people used to survive, and thrive in relationship—by gathering together to grow, harvest, and put up food; to raise barns; to sew quilts; and so many other things that would be extremely difficult to do without the help of others. We found the interdependency we had experienced satisfying and heart-warming.

The etymology of "depend" gives us a rich context. The word comes from the PIE root *(s)pend-*, an extension of *(s)pen-* which means "to pull, draw, or stretch." The Middle French and Latin forms of "depend" (*dependre* and *dependere*, respectively) mean, "to hang from, hang down, be suspended," and this is where "pendant" comes from. Very closely related, and from the same root, is the word "span." The verb form of this word comes from the Latin word *pondus,* which means "weight," and may be referring to the weight of something and how much it stretches the cord from which it hangs. The image of pendant comes to mind again. The noun form of the word "span" in Old English means "to join, link, clasp, fasten, bind, connect, stretch;" and in Middle Dutch it means "stretch, bend, hoist, hitch."

The addition of *inter-* is to highlight and emphasize the reciprocal nature of dependency that the indigenous soul needs and fosters. Its PIE root *enter* means "between, among." Interdependence is what connection looks like in action. It means pulling one end of the boat back up so that the whole boat doesn't go down.

Three features of interdependence are worth examining. The first is what Martin Prechtel calls "indebtedness," and he describes it thusly: "The idea is to get so entangled in debt that no normal human can possibly remember who owes whom what, and how much. This assures that no one will be an orphan."[12] Precthel is referring to the indigenous or village understanding that we are responsible to each other, and to the welfare of the collective. To allow one person to fail, starve, or stray is to threaten the whole group. To let one end of the boat sink is to let all drown together.

Prechtel's definition flies in the face of our 21st century America's (or any other Westernized country's) experience with debt, and its intimate relationship with the value we place on independence. We've been well trained to remain as debt-free as possible, or to get out of debt as soon as possible.

Two aspects of debt point out the glaring differences between the indigenous vs. the Westernized perception of indebtedness. One is the source of debt, and the other is the terms. In Westernized cultures, the source of one's debt is typically one or more individual entities (person, service provider, or institution) that the debtor relies on for episodic or ongoing assistance. In contrast, the indigenous understanding of debt covers one's entire existence, not just on occasions when some assistance is needed. According to Prechtel: "The knowledge that every animal, plant, person, wind, and season is indebted to the fruit of everything else is an adult knowledge. To get 'out of debt' means you don't want to be part of life, and you don't want to grow into an adult."[13]

From an indigenous perspective, every person is born into a state of indebtedness, because each of us owes our very existence to whoever brought us into this world, and our debt accumulates thereafter for the rest of our lives, because the source of our debt now includes not only the spirit and ancestral world that brought us here, but the whole village that now sustains us.

As for the terms of indebtedness, debt in the village is not paid back, but forward. Just as you needed help today, so will someone else need your help tomorrow. Contrast that with our culture of capitalism, where we pay back the individual we borrowed from, in order to be free of any further obligation.

Essentially, it is the difference between *gift* and *loan*. Gifting is the currency of indigenous economics. Loaning is not, because it excludes the rest of the collective. A gifting and indebted economy ultimately reaches everyone in the village, but a loan is limited to two or three people, operating in a closed interaction. To exclude is to make an outsider or stranger, thereby weakening the web of connection due to lack of trust. Usury—the depersonalization and spiritual castration of money—is not far behind. Stephen Jenkinson sums it up: "The spirit of usury (self-interest) is contrary to the spirit of community (mutual obligation)."[14] Only the lender, never the community, reaps benefits of usury. In his book, *Sacred Economics*, Charles Eisenstein states it this way:

> When every economic relationship becomes a paid service, we are left independent of everyone we know and dependent, via money, on anonymous, distant service providers. That is a primary reason for the decline of community in modern societies, with its attendant alienation, loneliness, and psychological misery.[15]

A second feature of interdependence, closely related to indebtedness, is that of sharing vs. accumulating. The indigenous soul knows that abundance comes not from accumulating personal wealth, but from sharing what you have with others. At a deeper level, it recognizes that personal ownership is a myth. Whatever degree or form of wealth exists is the result of community-wide effort and also blessings from the spirit realm. Wealth must be shared with the collective, and with the spirit realm. So strong is this ingrained in village life that hoarding is considered to be a far more serious crime than murder. While we may see examples of such interdependency in our Westernized culture, it is not the norm. Our economy's health is measured by production and consumption of goods, and our big box stores and sprawling storage units are temples honoring the god of surplus.

The third feature of interdependence is that of cooperation vs. competition. Competition yields one winner, and many losers. Why does it warm our hearts so when we watch an athlete forego her certain victory in order to drop back and assist a faltering competitor? Because the indigenous soul recognizes that when everyone works together toward a common goal, everybody wins! Further, the indigenous soul values each individual's unique contribution to the web of interconnections, and thus knows that such a connection would disintegrate rapidly without cooperation. "It's not a competition," writes Carlos Barrios. "The reality is that we all need each other. Our differences create balance."[16]

Reflect

1. Compare and contrast the times you were carrying debt and the times you were free of debt. What were the positives and negatives of each that you have experienced?
2. Did you ever receive a loan that made you feel loved and supported?
3. Reflect on a significant experience in your life in which you felt you had to *compete* against others in order to succeed. Was that a positive or negative experience, and why?
4. Next, reflect on an experience in which you felt you had to *cooperate* with others in order to succeed. Was that a positive or negative experience, and why?

Practice

To honor our natural state of interdependence, we must look for ways to practice indebtedness, sharing, and cooperation in our daily lives. The web of interconnectedness is infinite, so where do we start? With whom can we practice and enhance our skills of interdependence? These questions lead to the next chapter.

5

BELONG

The sound most similar to a newborn's scream is the sound of children, which is why children in my village are required to cry out in confirmation of the newborn's arrival. What would happen to the newborn if there were no answer? Can infants recover from the damage done to their souls as a result of a message at birth that they are on their own?

−Malidoma Some´

The verb "belong" comes from the Old English word *langian*, which means, "pertain to, to go along with." The adjective "long" originates from the PIE root *dlonghos-*, which is the source of the Latin word *longus* (meaning "long, extended; further; of long duration; distant, remote"), Proto-Germanic *langgaz*, and Old English *lang*, "having a great linear extent, that extends considerably from end to end; tall; lasting."

Belonging means being pertinent to, related to, and thus important to. "Pertain" comes from the Latin word *tenere*, which means "to hold." The prefix *pre-* means "through." To belong is to be connected through being held; to be held, throughout. No matter how distant or remote you may feel, belonging means coming from a long line of others who hold you, through whatever circumstances arise.

To whom do we belong?

Because the animal world often mirrors human behavior to us in endearing ways, let's look at elephants as a starting point for answering that question. Rona Tyndall writes,[17] "Elephants form complex multi-generational societies in which tradition is passed from one generation to the next," where the elders initiate the adolescents into adulthood. They ritually grieve and mourn their dead, and bury them at a site that they return to annually to honor and remember.

Tyndall then describes the societal disruption caused by poaching and the loss of their natural environment, shredding the social fabric that is so necessary for the remaining young elephants to mature. As their parents are killed for their tusks, and their habitat is destroyed around them, the young elephants are stripped of all direction. "When baby elephants don't know who they belong to," Tyndall explains, "they don't know how to be in the world. When their natural, communal life-style is destroyed, elephants, like people, have no culturally enforced boundaries of behavior; they have no society to teach them how to become what they are meant to be."

Like elephants, without the guidance of our elders and the stability of a community in which to grow and learn, we cannot discern *who* we are (our true selves and our unique purposes) or *whose* we are (where we came from, and the meaning our placement in the trajectory of human life). The inevitable result is mayhem.

"It takes a village," the African proverb proclaims, and it is true of raising children and, more broadly, of fostering belonging throughout the village, and within each person. Villages are necessarily inter-generational and their members are cooperative, interdependent, and collectively responsible. We belong to our parents and our children, our grandparents and our grandchildren, our ancestors, and our descendants. We belong to colleagues, neighbors, classmates, and teammates, to all we co-operate with.

In our global village, we belong to all of humanity: "Everything is encoded in the gene pool," writes Joseph Rael. "Each human being is in the psyche of every other human being so that there isn't one of those human beings that is alone. Even though they never meet each other, they're still very much in each other."[18]

We not only belong to other people, we belong to the land. Once again, some additional etymological investigation yields treasure. The verb "land" has several meanings: (1) to belong; (2) to bring to land, to come to shore, to disembark (originally of ships, then later of airplanes); and (3) to make contact, to hit home (a blow). Figuratively, these describe our birthplaces as predetermined, non-random sites.

The noun form of "land" supports these notions with its own meanings: home region of a person or people; solid surface of the earth; and the abode of humans, as opposed to the heavens or the underworld. While the creation of Adam (man) from dust (land) is one of the most well-known, many other primal myths of creation identify earth or dirt as an original ingredient of humanity. At how many funerals have we been reminded, "From dust we came, to dust we shall return?" And in between our origins and endings in dust, we are intimately connected with the land, as Joseph Rael indicates:

> The land is who we are. The land is our first significant energy, which we begin to recognize as ourselves. The land is where our power really lies and that is where expanded consciousness can be cultivated. When anything is occurring, in any moment in time, it is occurring not only to the individual, but also to that geography. We are in constant energy exchange with Earth.[19]

This primal truth resides in every indigenous soul. That truth awakens in us every time we plant seeds and harvest their fruit later, and every time we bury a deceased loved one in the ground. We belong to the land.

We are inter-connected, and inter-dependent; and we belong to each other. What does this mean to us, and what does it look like in practice?

Reflect

1. Recall a group that you used to or currently belong to. What is it about the group that made/makes you feel like you belong?
2. Does a sense of connection to a people or a place require some time to develop, or can connection be felt instantly? Or both? Reflect on examples of each in your own life experiences.
3. Where were you born? Do you still live there? Do you feel a connection to your birthplace? Why or why not?

Practice

1. Belong yourself to others.
    *   Compassionately engage in cooperative and responsible ways that emulate and build yours and others' unique humanness.
    *   Give and receive genuinely and generously.
    *   Hold up others, and let them hold you up.
    *   Commit yourself to the greater good of the line as you lengthen it by one.
    *   Let your position in this line melt any reluctance you have to being present and engaged with others. Let it reassure you that you and the contributions you make are needed.

- Hear yourself say as you hold, "I'm needed, and important." Hear yourself say as you are held, "I'm connected, and supported."

2. Belong others to you.
   - Call them yours. Claim them as your kin (from the same PIE root as "indigenous," *gene*, "to produce"), for you have the capacity to produce a longer line of belonging. Put no limits on who is befitting of a place in line, for belonging others to you is an inclusive process, not an exclusionary one.
   - Challenge yourself to make room in the line especially for those whom you fear (warranted or not)—this will help chase away any feelings of unimportance or loneliness that both of you may be carrying.

3. Belong the land to you. Mother Earth already and instinctively knows that we belong to Her. She has called us her children since the beginning of humanity. She longs for the relationship to be reciprocal. Chapter 12 covers this relationship in more detail.

4. Celebrate your successful practice.

5. Repeat as needed.

6

LEARN

When you see a new trail, or a footprint you do not know,
follow it to the point of knowing.

–Uncheedah (Grandmother of Ohi'ye S'a)

The etymology of "learn" takes us in an unpredictable direction, yet a very fitting one when you think about it. Learn comes from the PIE root *leis*, which means "track, furrow," which is related to the German word *Gleis* ("track"), to Old English *læst* ("sole of the foot"), and to the noun form of "last," which means "track, footprint, footstep, trace."

Origins of "last" are Proto-Germanic *laist*, Old Norse *leistr* ("the foot"), Dutch *leest* ("form, model"), and Old High German *leist* ("track, footprint"). From these origins, we discover that learning is a journey we take one step at a time, observing every footprint and bend in the furrow before us.

In comparison, "know" comes from the PIE root *gno* ("to know"), from which come the Old English roots *cnawan* ("perceive a thing to be identical with another; be able to distinguish"), and *tocnawan* ("perceive or understand as a fact or truth," as opposed to "believe").

A notable contrast between "learn" and "know" is in their

different goals: learning is process-focused, but knowing is outcome-focused. The goal of learning is following tracks to see where they take you; the goal of knowing is finding the animal that made the tracks.

The indigenous soul knows that learning is a *being fed* experience, not an *eating* one. It's a growth process, not an accomplishment. Learning is the very purpose of our lives. Earth is our classroom, and we are lifelong students. Carlos Barrios says, "This is the story of Mother Earth and us as her children. This is the planet's purpose."[20]

Each one of us has come to earth to learn specific lessons for this particular lifetime. Our souls took on physical bodies in order to learn how to live in a physical world. "We come here to manifest," Joseph Rael reminds us. "We agreed to come down, and by the time we were born we had already been given a place on the planet. We were born to fulfill a vision, and all the trials and tribulations are exercise, to make us the best possible conduits to move energy through the world, to enhance creation."[21]

To each of us, situations present themselves that are designed specifically for us to learn the certain lessons meant uniquely for us in this lifetime. These "catalysts of joys and sorrow"[22] are our teachers. Our purpose is to understand these catalysts as lessons, not punishment or transgression against us. If the same catalyst or teacher seems to be showing up again and again, it's an indication that the lesson has not yet been learned sufficiently. With each lifetime we experience, we learn more lessons, all of which steer us to our graduation—to a higher level of understanding of what it means to be human.

"It's hard work, being alive," a colleague told me once, and we both chuckled at the humor and truth of it. Learning costs us. It asks us to venture outside our comfort zones, and to anticipate being radically changed. Nicolya Christi, author of several books on the current planetary shift, warns us that learning involves discomfort: "You are on existing Earth to learn compassion, empathy, understanding and unconditional love, through the experience of suffering [which literally means "enduring, carrying"]."[23]

We give up much when we accept the challenge to learn: the comfort of our pre-tracking position; our limited understanding and biased perceptions of how the cosmos works and of our place in it; and our intimate relationship with our egos. Learning involves yielding to wisdom and experience far greater than ours, and letting go of our faulty perceptions and expectations. It is an initiation process that requires us to grow up and get wise.

What do we get when we follow the learning track? Our learning! Learning costs us, but it also rewards us. We learn details, good and bad, about our personal and ancestral history, thereby discovering from whom we come and to whom we return. We learn the origins of things (food, language, practices, beliefs, and more) and their interrelationships. We learn the natural partnership between the seen and the unseen worlds, and the multi-dimensionality of ourselves. We learn how to be fully human. It's hard work, but worth it!

Reflect

1. As you reflect on some of your most memorable learning experiences, what was easy for you to learn, and why?
2. What was difficult to learn (and perhaps still is), and why?
3. How has learning helped you discern your life's purpose?
4. In what ways has learning "cost" you?

Practice

1. Initiate conversation with people whose life experiences are dramatically different from yours.
2. For every favorite source of information that you rely on (i.e., written media, websites, persons, broadcasts, etc.), research

and explore a contrasting source or viewpoint, and spend some time with it.

3. When you learn something that seems untrue or unbelievable, be curious rather than suspicious, and "follow the trail."

4. Explore the social, political, historical, and cultural context of the sources of your learning.

5. Celebrate your successful practice.

6. Repeat as needed.

7

REMEMBER

*The Remembering is the gradual unfoldment of the Spiritual Essence within
each person. It takes form when human beings come fully alert, aware of all
that has come before, their rightful place in Creation, and choice of paths
the Great Mystery gave them.*

–Jamie Sams

The word "remember" is a composite of *re-* (meaning, "again") and
member, which comes from the Latin *memorari*, meaning, "be mindful
of." This Latin word is related to "memory," whose PIE root *(s)mer*
means "remember." Other words with this same root have related
meanings, including "mindful, care, thought, ponder;" and "anxiety,
sadness, remember sorrowfully."

Where learning is about discovering something you don't yet
know, remembering is about discovering something that you forgot
you knew. Remembering is putting back together what has come
loose, detached, or separated.

The opposite of remember is not "forget;" it's "dismember."
Remembering is primarily the work of the mind as it confronts the
illusion of disconnection. It is the combination of our emotional,
mental, and spiritual dimensions *re-minding* us of our eternal,

unbreakable connection to everything else. This is the mindful, caring, thoughtful, pondering nature of remembering.

The other feature of remembering revealed in its etymology is anxiety, sadness and sorrow. Perhaps the most obvious or familiar experience of these feelings of remembering is when we are grieving what used to be. We miss a certain person or that house or those times. Our sadness is a result of us perceiving a permanent disconnect from something or someone so dear to us. But given enough thought and care, our minds will remember that our beloveds are not gone and not disconnected, but merely present in a different form.

Like learning, remembering can be uncomfortable. Both challenge, or even shatter our perceptions of reality, forcing us to re-examine what we thought was true. Letting go of a fast-held belief is at least unsettling, if not traumatic. As more and more old beliefs fall to the wayside, the spell of disconnection is broken. Like learning, remembering is a growth process, a maturation, an initiation, and thus a vital part of our Earth-school experience. Remembering is a skill that we will need to practice in this new age, as formerly unknown truths are being disclosed.

The primary focus of our remembering is ourselves. This has nothing to do with individualism or self-reliance; in fact, it is the antithesis of these things. Rather, it is important for each of us to remember the unique purpose of our lives, so that we each know our specific role in the collective.

Generally speaking, the indigenous perspective shares the following common understandings about who we are, where we came from, and why we're here:

- Our lives are not random occurrences. Each of us was intentioned here by our ancestors, by the gods, by Creator, by Source, by the Holies . . . whatever term you want to use.
- Before we incarnated to earth, each of us, in our soul forms, collaborated and entered into agreement with the Holies about what our unique purpose was to be in that lifetime. *Purpose* doesn't mean *job* or *task*, but *person*. We each incarnate

to find out who we are in that lifetime, and what we are to offer of ourselves to the collective good.

- The agreement covered the lessons we are to learn in order to accomplish our unique purpose to become that unique person, and it included the people and the events that were necessary to create situations for us to learn our lessons.

- Most of us have had at least one previous lifetime on Earth. Most of us will have more Earthly lifetimes after our current one. Each lifetime carries with it a new sacred contract.

- Each of us is a multi-self, a non-incarnate collection of all our past lives. The multi-self remembers all the lessons from all our previous lifetimes, but our human forms on earth do not. The lessons we learned in previous lives are checked off the list, such that we do not need to learn them again in a new life. With each new life incarnation comes new lessons, ones we haven't learned in previous lives. This cycle doesn't go on forever; there is an end-point. But there are *many* lessons.

Every circumstance in our lives—no matter how good or bad; no matter how inconsequential it may seem—is part of our remembering curriculum. If situations in your life have caused you to think or say, "I didn't sign up for this," in fact, you did. Everything that happens to us is part of our sacred contracts, which we agreed to before we were born here. Some lessons are enjoyable to learn, some are difficult, and some are downright excruciating. Everyone has some of each of these in their lifetime experiences. What is asked of each of us is to remember that everything that happens to us in our lives is for our own learning and growth, directed by our sacred contracts. This presents a challenge for us, but also a gift: it helps us to make meaning of our life experiences even when they're not fun and even when they don't seem to make any sense. Either way, the best thing we can do is ask ourselves, "What's the lesson here for me?" The more we accept this challenge, the sooner we learn our lessons, and the less homework we continue to have!

How do lessons help us remember who we are? Each lesson

offers some information to us that we can add to our accumulation of self-knowledge. It takes years to remember who we are! The more lessons we experience, the more information we gather, and the more we can discern who we are and what our purpose is in this life. This happens through preserving and continuing attitudes or practices that present our best selves and serve the better interests of others, and eliminating those that don't. Over time, if we're paying attention, each of us will be successful in creating a spiritual résumé that coheres more and more with the sacred contract we made before we were born.

There are personal and communal rewards of remembering the who, where, and why of our lives. Personally, remembering who we are is the antidote to self-doubt, self-hate, low self-esteem, and other feelings of unworthiness that are pervasive in our culture. Such deprecating opinions about ourselves indicate that we've missed the opportunity to see our mistakes as lessons for learning, and instead saw them as failures. Until we are ready to say "Oh, I get it!" instead of "I'm so stupid!," the same lessons will recycle through our lives until we are ready to learn from them. Collectively these lessons are designed to help us realize how beautiful and whole and perfect we naturally are. The goal of our earthly incarnations is to remember that.

The communal benefit of remembering manifests itself in shapes and forms of the village. The inter-dependency feature of the village works to bolster each individual as well as the collective. As a whole, the village's responsibility is to help each individual village member to discover and practice the genius that lies within. The strength and unity of the village depends on each individual's purpose being manifested. Think of the block-stacking game called Jenga—it's a matter of time before the removal of even one block will bring the whole tower crashing down. As every block is needed for a stable and durable tower, so is every person needed for a robust community, planet, and cosmos.

Reflect

1. Have you ever felt like you have lived one or more lives prior to your current life? How might your previous lives relate to this one?

2. Reflect on the "A-ha" moments you have had when you heard something seemingly for the first time, yet its instant resonance with you made you respond, "Yes, of course." or "I knew it!"

3. Have you discerned what your unique purpose in this life is? When did you start to get a sense of it? Has your sense of this purpose shifted over time?

4. Reflect on a painful or even traumatic event or situation in your life that you can now look back on and say, "If *that* hadn't happened to me, I wouldn't have had *this* opportunity to . . . ."

Practice

1. Consider these resources to help you remember who you are and why you're here on Earth:

   • **Astrology** – Based on the placement and movement of planets and stars and other celestial bodies in the sky on the day, time, and place of your birth, a great deal of information about not only your current life but also some past life experiences can be revealed. Your astrological chart can reveal what lessons are primary for you in this lifetime, as well as formative episodes in your current lifetime and hints toward your future.

   • **The Maya Cholq'ij Calendar** – Where astrological readings focus on a snapshot of time on the date, time, and place of one's birth, the Maya Cholq'ij takes into account the rhythms of Earth and the cosmos, and how the human body is wired into those energies. Carlos Barrios says of this calendar: "This instrument allows each of us to find our place in the world, understand our propensities, strengths, and weaknesses, and lead an existence that is in harmony with our individual life purpose and thus reach our full potential, guiding our physical, intellectual, emotional, and spiritual growth."[24] The Cholq'ij calendar is useful in learning our unique purpose, gifts, and personalities; and it also provides daily guidance based on the energies of the day. (See Chapter 32 and Appendix A for more information.)

- **Sacred Contracts** – Author and medical intuitive Carolyn Myss developed a tool for determining one's sacred contract with the universe, the agreement in which each soul participates with the spiritual realm prior to incarnation. In her book, *Sacred Contracts: Awakening Your Divine Potential*,[25] Myss describes the importance of seeing our lives symbolically—archetypically, in particular—in order to know better why we are here and how we are to use our personal power for the betterment of our relationships and ourselves. The Sacred Contract tool she developed includes the Archetypal Wheel and a Gallery of Archetypes, designed to help us create and interpret our own charts of origin.

- **Shamanic Divinations** – Shamans, using a variety of ancient techniques, act as advocates in the spiritual realm, on behalf of a person who is seeking healing or other spiritual direction to regain holistic balance. Through a variety of techniques, shamans are able to get answers about a particular situation the client is facing, a particular question that the client has, or even about the client's future.

- **Sacred Path Cards**[26] **and Medicine Cards**[27] – Both of these book and cards kits offer spiritual guidance pertaining to given times or situations, and generally toward a better understanding of one's true self and the path it is on. The information in the *Sacred Path* kit comes from Native American stories and rituals, and the *Medicine Card* kit provides knowledge and wisdom gained from what animals can teach us about Animal Medicine, and ourselves.

2. Celebrate your successful practice.
3. Repeat as needed.

8

INTUIT/DREAM

Everyone who is successful must have dreamed of something.

–Native American Maricopa Proverb

To "intuit" and to "dream" are not the same thing, but they are inseparable co-workers in the life of a human being. "Intuit" means to "look at, consider, tutor." "Tutor" means "private teacher, watcher, guardian." The PIE root of "intuit" and "tutor" is *teue*, meaning, "pay attention to." With the *in-* prefix, intuit might originally mean something like, "pay attention to what's inside;" or "that which is inside teaches."

Swep-, the PIE root of the verb "dream," means "to sleep." Thus, the working relationship between "intuit" and "dream" may be expressed in this way: That which is inside you (intuition) watches, and privately teaches you while you sleep (dream).

Because "instinct" is often used synonymously with "intuition," its etymology is worth examining as well, for the purpose of contrast. "Instinct" is comprised of *in-* ("into, inside") + *stinguere*, from the PIE root *steig*, which means, "to prick, stick, pierce." The verb "to stick," from the same PIE root, has multiple meanings: "to remain embedded, stay fixed, be fastened;" and "to remain in place, to quilt.'"

38

Here is how these three words can be distinguished:

- **Instinct** remains imbedded inside you. It stays fixed, fastened to you. It's a survival skill for living in a physical world.

- **Intuition** is more transitory, serving as a bridge between the 3rd Dimension and higher Dimensions.

- **Dreaming** is your spiritual component, your soul, reaching beyond the confines of your physical body. It is a 4th Dimension and higher phenomenon. ("Dimensions" are explained in greater detail in the Balance and Coordinate chapters, and illustrated in the Appendix.)

Imagine a place where everything there is to learn and understand can be found . . . like the Internet, but infinitely larger, and completely truthful. Then imagine that you had a lifetime, round-trip ticket to visit that place whenever and as often as you wanted. The great news is this: you don't have to imagine or wish it. This place does exist and you have unlimited access to it. It's called the Dream World, and your ticket is your own intuition.

With the exception of those who have taken workshops and received training in dream interpretation, most Westernized folks have a limited understanding of what dreaming is about. Many have little interest in, and perhaps give no credence to, the value of dreams. This is evident in some of the most common statements heard about dreams:

"Did I dream that, or was it real?"

"Dream on! That's never gonna happen!"

"I never remember my dreams." Worse yet, "I never dream."

Certainly in the past several decades there has been a significant rise in the interest in dreams and what they reveal to us, matched by a huge increase in the availability of resources devoted to this topic.

Gradually it has become more acceptable to talk about and give credence to our natural, albeit underdeveloped, intuitive abilities. Anymore, gut feelings and hunches are considered legitimate sources of guidance. I hope that a similar gain in respect for daydreaming will happen soon, but that would require a mammoth reduction in the speed and busy-ness of our daily lives.

Deja-vu episodes—moments that we feel we've lived through before—are common experiences that are routinely accepted as real, not imaginary. Daydreams (dreaming while awake), night dreams (dreaming while asleep), and déjà-vu experiences are all messages from higher dimensions of ourselves than the 3rd Dimension physical realm that we inhabit. They are the most common forms of out-of-body experiences that we have available to us that give us access to our higher dimensions.

Clairvoyance (the ability to see visions or images from the spiritual realm), clairaudience (the ability to hear things from other realms), and clairsentience (the ability to feel messages from other realms such as fluctuations in energy flow) are all intuitive practices. Some people have highly developed intuition, others very little. But every human being has intuition and is capable of utilizing it to perceive things that are not detectible in the physical world by our five senses.

As stated earlier, intuition is your ticket to other realms or Dimensions of existence. If you think of movies like *Avatar* and *The Matrix*, the notion of different Dimensions is comprehensible. The great planetary shift that is happening now is due to Earth's evolutionary rise from the 3rd Dimension (physical realm) into the 4th Dimension, and ultimately into the 5th Dimension. Most human beings dwelling on Earth are primarily living in the 3rd Dimension, but they frequently visit the 4th Dimension or higher during awake-dreaming and asleep-dreaming. The more spiritually evolved among us operate out of the higher Dimensions without requiring a dream state. But for most of us, the dream state is the most common avenue for us to access higher Dimensions.

The higher Dimensions, the 5th and above, are the homes of spirit guides of all kinds: animal spirits, ancestors, angels and archangels, saints, the risen Christ, and a host of other non-physical beings. People's recollection of their dreams often include descriptions of some of these very beings. As our dreams carry us into the higher dimensions, divine guidance from these non-physical beings becomes available to us. It's up to us to investigate what the appearances of those dream characters mean, so that we can discern the guidance they offer us. I regularly investigate the spiritual significance of beings (e.g., animals) or situations (e.g., a tidal wave that overtook but didn't faze me) that were in my dreams. From the assorted interpretations, I reflect on my life and intuit what the message or guidance is for my unique situation.

The indigenous soul is the ultimate frequent flyer! Its comfort zone is in the flying—in the shuttling back and forth between dimensions. The indigenous soul knows how interdependent the higher and lower dimensions are in keeping both the awake world and the sleeping world alive. It knows that these two worlds are two sides of the same coin, that what one world dreams actually manifests in the other world. Here's how the Aboriginal myth goes:

> Humanity and all the world dreams, and through these dreams continually receive the potencies of the Ancestors. With equal constancy humanity returns the power to them in daily life, in song, in ritual and dance. Our tangible world is nothing other than the Dreaming of the Ancestors. Reciprocally, our desires, dreams, and inner activities of mind are the embodied life of the Ancestors. Human dreams, human creations, take place within a Great Dream

that is already complete. We are dreaming within a Dreaming.[28]

Maya Shaman Martin Prechtel offers this additional description of the relationship between these two worlds:

> When you dream, you remember the Other World, just as you did when you were a newborn baby. When you're awake, you're part of the dream of the Other World. In the "waking" state, I am supposed to dedicate a certain amount of time to feeding the world I've come from. Similarly, when I die and leave this world and go on to the next, I'm supposed to feed this present dream with what I do in that one. Dreaming is about the person feeding the whole, remembering the Other World, so that it can continue.[29]

The awake world and the dreaming world have an interdependent, reciprocal relationship. Shamans encourage us to acknowledge and honor the power of dreaming.

Our indigenous souls remember that in the Dream World are messages that inform us about who we are, and that guide us in day-to-day life. What and whom we dream about is not random but is synchronistic. Our dreams are messages for us personally. When we dream, our souls journey to other realms intentionally, and beings from the Dream World come and meet us with tailor-made wisdom.

"Dreams read life back to us like a storyteller," Prechtel tells us. "They are a direct, incorruptible expression of the mysterious nature of life, and are considered to be free of human connivance."[30]

Dreaming is a skill that each of us can develop to enhance our souls' inter-dimensional travels, refresh our bodies, and bring more meaning into our lives. Dreams are also a dress rehearsal for future events in our lives, especially our time of death, when the spirit leaves the body for good. Practicing dreamtime prepares each of us to face our death without fear.

Dreams invite us into the higher dimensions of ourselves, inform us of our relationship with the spirit world, and inspire us to embrace the unseen as an intimate partner of the seen. The mystery of our lives calls us to be dreamers.

Reflect

1. John Lennon famously sang, "You may say I'm a dreamer, but I'm not the only one." Are you a dreamer?
2. Do you like to daydream? Why or why not?
3. Reflect on some memorable dreams you've had. How did they make you feel? What information did they provide to you?

Practice

1. Accept the responsibility of dreaming the continuation of life.
2. Establish a daily spiritual practice that includes some quiet, undisturbed time.
3. Pay attention to symbols and signs in your daily life (day dreams).
4. Trust and develop your clair- (-voyant, -sentient, -audient) skills.
5. Pay attention to your dreams; write them down as soon as you awake so that you can remember them.
6. Share nighttime dreams with others. Form a group that meets with you to do this very thing. Indigenous populations have treasured this daily practice for centuries. Where these days we turn on the TV or check the internet first thing in the morning, our indigenous counterparts gather around the fire and share dreams. What they learn from each other's dreams is the most important news there is. That same type of news is available to us.

7. Dreaming is actually a shamanistic practice. Anyone who dreams is shaman-ing! Research shamanic practices (e.g., drumming) that can help you enter the Dream World.
8. Research, learn and practice the skills of active dreaming.
9. Do some research on spirit guides to learn about their wide variety of forms and functions.
10. Celebrate your successful practice.
11. Repeat as needed.

9

PLANT

Every morning I turn my face to the wind and scatter my seed. It is not difficult to scatter the seeds, but it takes courage to go on facing the wind.

–Arab Proverb

I once had a neighbor across the street who was an old, white-haired man, living by himself. Thin and weathered, he walked with a cane, and his shoulders were stooped. Among the stories he told me were the ones of his younger days when he and his family grew up dirt-poor, relying almost exclusively on the food that they raised themselves. All of his life he gardened, because if his family didn't garden, they didn't eat. Even in his elder years, he still managed a very small plot, containing less than a dozen tomato plants. During the summers, he would keep me regularly supplied with tomatoes, so much so that I could hardly eat them as fast as he replenished them.

Once I asked, "Why don't you can or freeze some of these so you can have them this winter?"

"Naw, I don't like tomatoes," he replied.

"What?!? You plant tomatoes every year and tend them, and you don't even like them? Why bother, then?"

"I been gardnin' all my life," he explained. "I wouldn't know how to live if I stopped plantin'. Besides, if there's seeds, I'll plant 'em. That's what they're for."

The verb "plant" comes from the Latin word *plantare*, meaning, "to insert firmly." Other meanings include "to drive in, or push into the ground, with the feet," from *planta* ("sole of the foot"). The PIE root is *plat-* which means, "to spread, flat." The noun form of "place" is closely related, with meanings of "courtyard, open space, broad way." A synonym of plant is "sow," which means, "to scatter seed upon the ground or plant it in the earth; disseminate." Sow comes from the same PIE root (*se-ti-*) as seed, semen, and season. These original meanings indicate that to plant is to insert firmly, as well as scatter, into a wide-open place. The use of our hands is a given; yet with its close connection to "foot," planting involves our feet as well. Both breadth (via hands) and depth (via feet) of seed dispersion are important.

"Why do you want life to continue?" our teacher asked. At first I thought this was a trick question, because the first answer that came into my mind was so obvious: "Because I'd rather be alive than dead." Then I realized that he wasn't talking about *my* life in particular, or any other single life. He was talking about life itself—life as action, as movement, as nature perpetuating itself. So I had to rephrase the question for myself: "Why do I want life to continue *even after my own death?*"

The closest I've ever come to confronting this question is the pondering of the meaning of life, but that's not the same thing. "What is the meaning of life?" is a question you answer on a philosophy test, or talk about with your friends over coffee or wine. "Why do you want life to continue?" is a question you answer to your unborn children and grandchildren.

To plant is to say "yes" to the continuation of life, even if you can't answer the "why" part. Further, to plant is to add, "How can I help?" to the "yes."

The good news for planters is that life's longing to continue resides in every seed. That same longing, which also exists in humans, moves us to put seeds into each other and into dirt, and to feed and water them with hope and prayer. Life's longing is relentless. Seeds are made to crack open and sprout. The volunteers that pop up in our gardens or compost piles testify to this truth. The natural perpetuity of life is encased in every seed. As such, seeds are eternity in our hands, blurring past, present, and future into one. They are children and grandchildren of parents who have since died (the past); ready in their current form to be planted (the present); and soon-to-be parents of the next generation of fruit and seeds (the future). Seeds repeatedly and forever say, "Yes."

From an indigenous perspective, seeds are heirlooms, prized items passed on to future generations. Seeds and their sowers and reapers have stories, and those too are passed down—accounts of droughts and floods; the bountiful years and the bleak ones; who had green thumbs and who didn't; the feasts that were enjoyed and by whom; the rituals performed and the recipes followed. All of these stories and more teach us the history of seeds and food, re-membering them to us and us to them. Like the sowers and reapers, the seeds and their stories are alive. Their partnership keeps life going.

In his extraordinary book, *The Unlikely Peace at Cuchumaquic*, Martin Prechtel eloquently writes about how to farm consciously, beautifully, responsibly . . . in short, *indigenously*. For me, there is one concept that he describes passionately that seems to cover it all, and that is courtship. I have learned through Prechtel's teachings that as a planter, I must court my garden like she is the love of my life. That means getting to know her like a would-be girlfriend. In the past few years I have been learning what she likes (attention, gifts, wooing) and dislikes (abuse, being taken for granted). Practically speaking this includes the use of natural, organic methods of farming that are healthy for the soil and plants and other forms of life; year-round attention, even in the cold months; the use of no-till and fallow methods of planting; and the planting of non-treated and non-GMO seeds.

In wooing her, I have enjoyed singing to her, playing music to her, dressing up for her, decorating her with prayer flags and other ornaments, and telling her constantly how absolutely beautiful she is. In honoring her, I ceremoniously enter into her space each spring to begin our partnership of growing. With reverence and commitment, I have buried gifts to her, in private rituals meant only for her. I now bless and blow a kiss to every plant or seed I place in her, asking her to accept these and be willing to grow them for the purpose of feeding my loved ones and me. I flatter her and her babies, the plants and their fruits.

When the time comes to pick the fruit, I petition her, "May it be so, Mother, that these your babies would be willing to die to this life to feed me? May it be so that you would be willing to nourish me thusly, so that I may in turn nourish and feed this very fine Creation of which I am a part?" And when the growing and harvesting seasons are over, I tuck her in for the winter with ceremony, song, offerings, and prayer.

From an indigenous perspective, planting means using more than our hands and feet, and it also means knowing that seeds don't always come from a plant. In the description of my own gardening practices, the use of my hands and feet is easy to imagine. Subtler, perhaps, is the planting I did with my voice and mind and heart. With every word spoken and song sung to my garden, I planted seeds of gratitude, love, and kinship. In every moment of speechless quiet, I planted seeds of wonder, awe, and humility.

As dwellers on Earth, everywhere is our garden, and every living thing (which is every thing!) is a growing plant. The indigenous soul knows that every thought, spoken word, and action from us is a dissemination of seeds. Just as the mighty oak tree is the manifestation of the acorn's thought, so is every physical thing in our environment the offspring of thought. The origin of everything that exists is thought. Thus every thought we conjure and every action we perform literally matters—it becomes matter. Every word we speak literally counts—it adds physical manifestation to an ongoing creation. In other words, it's impossible for us *not* to plant.

Let us face *that* wind every day with courage by using our very best planting practices. Let us say "Yes!" to the continuation of life as we plant our very best seeds.

Reflect

1. Why do you want life to continue?
2. What seeds have you planted today with your hands, your feet, your voice, and your thoughts?

Practice

1. Take a moment to observe closely the seeds in your dietary fruits and vegetables. See them as the plant world's insistence that life goes on, rather than merely as inedible waste.
2. Plant some seeds, and follow their cycle of life over several generations. Harvest the second-generation seeds, and plant some of them. Give reverent attention to the dying of the first generation while you hold the seeds of the next one.
3. Walk and talk as if your total way of being in the world is an act of planting.
4. Plant your own garden, and nurture the relationship you have with it.
5. Celebrate your successful practice.
6. Repeat as needed.

10

BURY

They say: "We leave you our deaths. Give them their meaning."

–Archibald MacLeish

You may be wondering why the Bury chapter follows the Plant chapter instead of the Die chapter. It is important to understand how "bury" and "plant" are one and the same. At first glance, they may appear to be opposites: to plant is to initiate new birth and growth; to bury is to handle the remains of a life that has ended. But the indigenous soul is aware that this relationship is not a polarized one, but a circular one.

Life leads to death, which feeds new life, which then dies, and so on. In order for seeds to generate new growth (germinate), they have to crack open and die. The seed form of life has to die to the plant form. For our modernized culture to remember this truth, we must see how this cycle plays out all around us and includes us.

This awareness is necessary for us to understand what it means to be fully human within that cycle, and ultimately what our own deaths mean. All the burials in which we participate throughout our lives serve as reminders of how our own deaths will feed the next cycle of life.

"Bury" comes from the PIE root *bhergh-*, "to hide, protect." Its Old English derivative *byrgan* means, "to raise a mound, hide, bury, inter." Other related original meanings include "to shelter, to preserve, to save." What is it that we are protecting, preserving, hiding when we bury? Let's look first at the seed example, and then we'll look at human life.

Many gardeners, including me, save seeds from year to year, from the fruits of our plants. The irony here is that, to truly save the seeds so that they continue on and on into perpetuity, we have to bury them. If we hang onto them for more than a few years, their likelihood of germinating is drastically reduced. At some point these seeds will completely lose their capacity to reproduce. That's why there's an expiration date on seed packets. Burying (planting) seeds protects and preserves the life/death cycle. Seeds unburied rupture the continuity of life.

The sanctity of the life/death cycle is also preserved via burial. Gardeners often claim that going into the garden is like going to church. From an indigenous perspective, standing in a garden is bearing witness to both the beauty and the heartache of this holy cycle. It is to balance our excitement about the new growing season with reverence for what will die out of necessity.

In the dirt-floored church of the garden, planting seeds becomes ceremony, a burial. To "bury" means, "to raise a mound." Every burial mound, then, is a small temple where the miraculous continuation of life is honored, and deaths are remembered. Gardens are burial grounds, hiding from our view the preservation of life.

In varying degrees, the same can be said of how we bury our dead and about the funerals we perform for our loved ones. Burial plots and mausoleums are the mounds we build to honor our human place in the cycle of life and death. We perform funerals to remember the deceased to us. But we also perform these rituals to take our places in the life/death cycle. One of our responsibilities within this cycle is to bury our dead in a life-perpetuating way.

From an indigenous standpoint, burying a loved one involves preparing both the ground and the body as a gardener prepares both the dirt and the seed. With his hands and his feet, the gardener makes the connection between seed and dirt, life and death; and he's up to his ankles in it.

The same is asked of us when we bury our loved ones, yet the preparation of the body and of the burial ground are no longer performed by us. We've relinquished these sacred tasks to mortuaries and cemeteries. But can a gardener call himself a gardener if he pays someone else to do the planting? To bury a body is to plant it back into the earth to organically decay into rich, microbe-filled, life-giving dirt. Of course, this natural process is dramatically slowed, if not arrested completely, when a sealed, metal casket is involved. A gardener doesn't wrap his seeds in aluminum foil prior to planting them, for he knows that the seeds need direct contact with air, water, and dirt in order to generate new life.

Our indigenous souls know that the deceased's body deserves the same honorable handling as seeds, and they long to restore and return such life-perpetuating burial practices to their rightful place: in the hands of family and friends. Fortunately, "green funerals," which are gaining in popularity, offer alternatives that reflect ancient, indigenous practices aimed at preserving the continuity of life.

Burying is the antithesis of discarding. Discarding means disregarding, dismembering. In its original and truest sense, burying is a re-membering enterprise. The above-ground demonstration of that statement is our intentional focus on remembering during funeral and memorial services. The literal aspect of re-membering—regaining and maintaining our connection with the dead—is exactly what we seek in our grief. Underground, that same reconnecting happens, as death nudges life to poke through the surface. To bury something is to insert it back into the cycle, or as Joseph Rael calls it, "returning it to the dream."[31]

To bury something in the ground ("inter") is to preserve the physical and spiritual recycling that naturally takes place. Burials are not endings; they are continuations. They feed the dream that is the cycle of life. To bury is to preserve connection with us, and to give meaning to that which has died. That is what all of life asks of us.

Reflect

1. Reflect on who and what you have ever buried in the ground.
   - Do you perceive them to be still living in some form?
   - Where were they buried, and why are those places sacred to you?
   - How have their burials contributed to the continuity of life?
2. Have you given thought to your own burial wishes?

Practice

1. Maintain a compost pile where you can dump all your plant-based remnants (table scraps, grass clippings, leaves, etc.), and let their decay nurture your gardens and flower beds.
2. Research green burial options in your area.
3. Enter into council with your loved ones, where all can share their thoughts and wishes about their own burials.
4. Celebrate your successful practice.
5. Repeat as needed.

11

FEEL

The pain you feel today is the strength you feel tomorrow.
For every challenge encountered there is opportunity for growth.

−Ritu Ghatourey

The etymological study in this chapter explores the distinctions and the relationships between "feel" and three other words that are conceptually, if not linguistically, related: "emote," "empathy," and "sympathy."

"Feel" comes from the PIE root *pal-* meaning, "to touch, feel, shake, strike softly." From this same root come the Old English *felan*, ("to touch or have a sensory experience of; perceive or sense something" and "have a mental perception"); and the Latin words *palpare* ("to touch softly, stroke") and *palpitare* ("to move quickly").

"Emote" comes from the Latin *emovere*, "move out, remove, stir up, agitate." "Move," from which *-mote* is derived, is from the PIE root *meue-*, "to push away, set in motion."

"Feel" and "emote" both denote movement, but the direction of the movement appears to be opposite: "feel" has an inward motion or internal location of perception, while "emote" has a distinct outward push associated with it. Another difference is that the sensation of "feel" appears to be more neutrally perceived while "emote" is more disturbing. To feel is to touch and perceive something; to emote is to stir something up and push it out.

Feeling presents us with a learning opportunity and sets the stage for a well-thought-out response. In contrast, emoting blocks any chance of higher learning about the stimulus, and yields a quick (i.e., non-contemplated) reaction.

The relationship between emoting and feeling is an interdependent one, and our chakra system is aligned to guide that relationship. Basically the 1st, 2nd, and 3rd chakras (which I refer to as "below the belt" chakras) are the energy centers that focus on physical safety and security, family and relationships, and self-esteem. The 4th-7th ("above the belt") chakras are involved with love, forgiveness, will power, intuition, wisdom, and spirituality. The lower chakras help us navigate our physical world and basic relationships, while the upper chakras assist us with more esoteric matters and relationships with the unseen world. Emoting is a 3rd density, lower chakra expression, and feeling is a 5th density, upper chakra expression. Emoting is necessary for us to experience before any higher chakra work can be done. Only when our lower chakras are satisfied that we're in no immediate danger can we shift the energy into the higher chakras, and transmute the emotional experience into a learning opportunity.

The goal is a higher chakra experience of feeling, but it cannot be achieved without a lower chakra experience happening first. The same is true for Dimensions, which are the planes or special locations surrounding our bodies, ranging in vibration frequencies. The goal is to achieve a higher (above-the-belt) frequency of vibration, indicating a higher level of consciousness in which you operate. The lower Dimensions and below-the-belt vibrations are necessary first steps in that progression. (More detailed information on Dimensions and Densities is provided in the Coordinate chapter and the Appendix.)

Our emotions can entrap us if we hold onto them and let them dictate how we go about our lives. According to shaman Alberto Villoldo, author of *One Spirit Medicine* and *The Four Insights*, unhealed emotions are stored in the luminous energy field. A shaman's role is to help the person get rid of toxic and lingering emotions, and replace them with feelings, which are real and fleeting. Essentially that process involves increasing the emotion's vibration level from 3rd to 5th density vibrations, and from lower chakras to higher chakras by intentionally processing the emotion and converting it to a growing pain.

Once our emotions are overcome, then our feelings are responses to stimuli that are catalysts to our learning. An indication that we have succeeded in learning is our ability to take note of what we've learned, move on unencumbered by any lingering emotions, *and* not be swayed off course when that same feeling is triggered again. The result is balance:

> This is not indifference or objectivity, but a finely tuned compassion and love, which sees all things as love. This seeing elicits no response due to catalytic reactions. Thus the entity is now able to become co-creator of experiential occurrences. This is the true balance. Balance is not indifference but rather the observer not blinded by any feelings of separation, but rather fully imbued with love.[32]

Another contrast between feeling and emotion is that feeling is present-oriented, while emotion is typically trapped in the past or projected onto the future. Once again this can be illustrated by their difference in densities (chakra vibrations) and dimension location.

Emotions operate from the lower chakras, which are all about personal and familial protection, security, and self-esteem. The perception of threat implies separation, as it operates from an "us-versus-them" mentality. An emotional reaction is based on fear. Stimuli that trigger emotions are either reviving past events that have not been resolved, or conjuring future events that potentially threaten one's sense of safety, security, and self-worth.

In contrast, feelings offer a learning opportunity in the present. In fact, the present is the only time in which such learning can occur.

When you choose to feel rather than emote, a teaching moment arises. Because feeling occurs at a higher chakra level than emoting does, you do not feel threatened. Instead, you can entertain it as a way to enhance your relationship with yourself, with others, and with your environment.

In summary, feelings operate in and foster love, not fear; connection, not separation; the present, not the past or future; and responsiveness, not reaction.

"Empathy" comes from the Greek word *empatheia* meaning, "passion, state of emotion." *Em-* is an assimilated form of *en* which means, "in, into;" and *-pathy* comes from *pathos*, meaning "feeling." The PIE root for *pathos* is *kwent(h)-*, which means "to suffer, endure." From that same source is the Old Irish *cessaim,* which means, "I suffer;" and also the Lithuanian *pakanta*, meaning "patience."

"Sympathy" comes from the Greek word *sympatheia* meaning "fellow-feeling, community of feeling." *Sym-* is an assimilated form of *syn,* which means "together;" and it comes from the PIE root *ksun-* meaning "with."

Both words deal with *pathos*, which means suffering or enduring. The difference in the two words boils down to their prefixes, and it may not be as subtle as it seems. Literally stated, to sympathize with someone is to suffer *with,* or suffer *together;* but to empathize with someone is to suffer *into.*

"I am with you while you suffer" is sympathy. Empathy is more intimate: "I feel your pain like you feel it." Deeper into: "We are one, in pain. There's no difference, no separation between us, in this pain." And finally: "I suffer *your* pain." In familiar words, "I walk in your moccasins."

Feelings of sympathy and empathy are spiritual stirrings within us that call us to discern the purpose of painful situations in life, and grow from them rather than be trapped by them. To engage in sympathy and empathy with someone in pain is to accept the invitation for such learning. This place of pain is not an ultimate destination, but a launch pad into remembering cosmic laws that increase our vibration and promote our ascension, such as All is One.

Delores Cannon, author of dozens of books on past life regressions, became convinced through her thousands of case studies that we humans come back to Earth's school over and over again to learn what it's like to be every form of life there is in order to learn that empathy. She claimed that it included every form of life that exists, from bug and worm all the way up to the most evolved creatures.

Apparently this is an indigenous notion as well: "When everyone has stood on every spoke of the Great Medicine Wheel and understands the feelings of the other Relations, we will have reached completion. Then the Tribes of Earth will no longer need the lessons that cause separation, for life will be united as one."[33]

Our feelings are one way in which our souls communicate with us. To honor our souls, then, is to let our feelings have their say, and to listen to them, and then let them go once we learn the lesson they came to teach us.

Reflect

1. Think of a recent stimulus (a.k.a., "catalyst for learning") in your life that triggered emotions or feelings to arise. Were you able to learn something from it, and then let your feelings soon dissipate? Or did you get stuck in your emotions?
2. Reflect on your significant relationships. Are any of them even partially reliant on the ongoing and shared experience of pain? If one of you said, "I'm not going to stay in that pain anymore. I've learned from it, and I'm moving upward and onward from it," what would happen to the relationship?
3. Consider a time that you felt misunderstood or unfairly judged. What was your greatest need at that time?

Practice

1. If someone says or does something hurtful to you, slowly count to 10 before responding. In that brief time, ask yourself: "Is there something here for me to learn about myself?" With that one question, you shift the attention away from the pain, and onto the teachable moment that is presenting itself to you.

2. Sometimes the emotions may be so strong that counting to 10 may not be enough to calm them. In this case, try emoting into a physical object (e.g., screaming into a pillow, crying into a towel, hitting a tennis ball or kicking a football), and then resume with the counting.

3. If you find yourself dwelling in the past or worrying about the future, take a few moments to stop what you're doing and thinking, and concentrate on the present. By getting grounded in this way, you are better equipped to utilize your higher chakras to convert your emotions into learning situations, and to alleviate your feelings.

4. Whenever you find yourself being critical or judgmental of someone, slowly count to 10 and ask yourself: "Do I know what they're going through? Have I walked a mile in their shoes?"

5. Celebrate your successful practice.

6. Repeat as needed.

12

WILD

You were wild once. Don't let them tame you.

−Isadora Duncan

The word "wild" is most commonly used as an adjective (e.g., the "Wild West") or a noun (e.g., going out into "the wild"). This chapter offers it as a verb, recommending actions that return us to our indigenous ways of living in harmony with Nature.

Old English forms of "wild" include *awildian* ("refuse to be tamed") and *wilde* ("in the natural state, uncultivated, untamed, undomesticated, uncontrolled"). The PIE root of wild is *welt-*, which means "woodlands; wild."

"Wild" is that which has not been managed or interfered with by humans, but instead left up to its own natural order and processes. Its location in the forest or woods indicates that "wild" is wherever humans have not moved in to live, and indeed where modern humans are strangers at best, uncomfortable and fearful at worst.

A similar word worth exploring is "veld." From the PIE root *pele-* ("flat, to spread"), veld (originally "feld") is an Old English precursor to "field," and it means "a parcel of land marked off and used for pasture or tillage;" and "plain, pasture, open land, cultivated land," as opposed to woodland. *Plane* ("flat surface, level, clear, even") comes from the same root. Veld in its original form is land that either naturally has no trees, or whose trees have been cut down to make way for pastures and gardens. Veld is the necessary buffer zone between the tamed and the wild spaces, and is described reverently by Martin Prechtel as "zones of peace, necessary for the continued health of the Wild in the face of human civilization."[34] The veld is a remembering place, he tells us:

> The veld was and should be a place of renewed memory that leaves the wild untouched and fed, and the people a little more wild and intact. For it is here in the veld that all the old rituals and community ceremonies came together, in groves of trees, at the base of old overgrown walls or granaries, at the springs in the veld's grasslands.[35]

To whom is the veld such an altar? Pagans.

In classical Latin, "pagan" means "villager, rustic; civilian, non-combatant;" and "of the country, of a village." It comes from *pagus*, related to *pangere*, which means, "to fix, fasten," from the PIE root *paq-* ("to fix"). From this same root comes the Latin word "pact" ("agreement, contract, covenant"), as well as the Sanskrit word "pasa" ("cord, rope") and the Greek word "pegnynai" ("to fix, make firm, fast or solid"). Pagans were the maintainers of the veld, the keepers of the agreement between the wild and the tame to co-exist interdependently and honorably. Our pagan ancestors remembered and celebrated the fixed cord that tied their lives to Mother Nature. This account, told by a San Bushman, testifies to that cord:

> If one day I see a small bird and recognize it, a thin thread will form between me and that bird. If I just see it but don't recognize it, there is no thin thread. If I go out tomorrow and see and really recognize the same

individual bird again, the thread will thicken and strengthen just a little. Every time I see and recognize that bird, the thread strengthens. Eventually it will grow into a string, then a cord, and finally a rope. This is what it means to be a bushman. We make ropes of all the aspects of the Creation in this way.[36]

Notably missing from the meanings of wild and veld is anything resembling home, or dwelling, because, of course, home is where humans live, not outside in the fields or forests. The indigenous soul is capable of thriving in human dwellings, as long as it is not deprived of its connection with the veld and with the wild. In pagan cultures throughout history and across the world, that connection was maintained and honored. But with the spread of monotheism that was often brutally enforced, paganism became demonized and nearly exterminated. The covenantal cord between humanity and nature was severed, and ritual moved indoors—into the homes and temples that we built—safe from the profanity of nature. As we crossed these thresholds and closed the doors behind us, we forgot.

We forgot the movements of the sun and moon and stars, and the cycle of seasons, relying on our linear-time calendars and clocks. We forgot how to feed and be fed by Mother Nature. We forgot that naturally occurring plant and animal life once offered food in abundance, so we cut it down and plowed it under to raise what we could to survive. We forgot that land and its inhabitants are alive, so we killed and excavated and called Earth a resource.

We forgot the natural cycle of death making way for life, so we devalued old age and defied our mortality. We forgot so much that we perceived Nature as a threat, becoming what Jamie Sams calls the "Afraid-of-Dirt" people: "The fear of dirt, dust, soil, and sand began to erode their sense of belonging to the Earth Mother."[37] With the cutting of our umbilical cords to Mother Nature, we forgot what we were born with—our indigenous souls.

No matter how domesticated we become, we cannot discard

our innate wildness. To ignore it is to risk becoming feral, the truly dangerous type of human wildness. Feral ("having escaped from domestication") is related to the word "fierce," which means "proud, noble, bold, haughty." Both come from the Latin word *ferus* ("wild, untamed, savage, cruel") and the PIE root *ghwer-* ("wild, wild animal").

Haughty, proud, cruel, and savage—these are not descriptive of Mother Nature; they are human characteristics, what humans become when we fail to uphold our part of the agreement to live in harmony with Her. They are what allow us to unconsciously abuse Her, in violation of our ancient covenant with Her. When we cut the cord between Nature and us, we lost the connection between the natural wildness that exists outside of our buildings and inside of our souls. Consequently, we've gone feral and She's gone hungry.

"Nature is still alive in us," Malidoma Some´ reminds us, "and that is why we feel nostalgia, or that we are in exile where we are. The call to come home to the natural world translates as feeling exiled, alienated, or maladjusted."[38] For the sake of Mother Nature and ourselves, we must "find our way back to the Garden," as the familiar folk song says. Nature is our home, and we are her children. It's time to commit ourselves to honoring the pact that our ancestors made with her and bequeathed to us to maintain.

Where shall we start?

First we grieve. We walk out the back door and into as natural a place as we can find, sit on the ground, put our faces into our hands, and sob-cry. The tears won't happen right away, but give it a few silent, phone-less, undistracted moments.

Let the earth under you nudge some ancient stirrings within you. Remember your childhood, when grass and dirt stains on your clothes were marks of intimacy, like lipstick on a collar. Observe how your breathing compliments the breeze, or is it vice versa? Now lay back and make an angel on the ground, as if there was snow beneath you. Then flip over and put your face in the grass and smell your

Mother. And remember. And then speak right into her skin, "I've missed you, Mother." And again, "Oh, how I've missed you!" And that ought to just about do it. Let the tears come, and let Mother hold you and ground you as you cry.

As we cry and bemoan our nostalgia, we must apologize to Mother Earth for our amnesia and our absence, and ask her for forgiveness. In reconciling our relationship with her, we must woo her, practicing courtship rituals much like the ones we conduct for our gardens. Remembering how indebted we are to Nature for our very lives, we must spare nothing of ourselves in this holy, homecoming moment!

Then, we need to revisit the pact, and familiarize ourselves with it all over again. For a very thorough and utterly poetic rendition of this pact, I refer you to Part IV of Martin Prechtel's book, *The Unlikely Peace at Cuchamaquic*. Of course, you'll need to read the first three parts to get the full meaning of Part IV, but you won't regret it.

A critical first step in revitalizing the pact is the restoration of the veld. No other steps will take hold unless we demarcate and honor the space to do so, and that space, as we have already determined, is the veld. That is where the dance floor is, the party place where the tame and tamed can commune with the wild in ways that are mutually beneficial and safe.

Most of us don't have acres of land that we can divide into three separate categories (domestic, veld, and wild), but wherever we are, we can put small-scale versions of this into practice. For example, instead of treating and manicuring your lawn to produce a homogenous, weed-less carpet of green, let flourish that which grows there naturally. The diversity of plant life will then sustain a diversity of insects and worms, which will then sustain a diversity of bird life, and so on. The official veld-ing of that natural lawn, then, requires a regular practice of ritual (fully described in Chapter 29) that re-members you and Nature to each other.

For those whose backyard consists of a 4th-story patio with assorted potted plants, see what grows voluntarily in the pot that you don't cultivate. If you simply do not have any landscape whatsoever to restore to veld, then visit and support wildlife preserves, national forests and the likes; and ritually feed them.

Veld-consciousness is what we need in order to be naturally, not ferally, wild. It will eliminate our fear of dirt, and invite us to go barefoot; yet it will also discourage us from taming what is better left wild. Only in that middle way of veld can we discern where our own wild stops, and Nature's wild begins.

The veld also offers us the best classroom to learn animal and plant Medicine. It is possible for us to remember the language of our plant and animal kinfolk, but it will require time well spent in the veld. Our ancestors relied on what Mother Nature taught them through Her wildlife, to the point of sacrifice. Antelope's speech, in *Other Council Fires*, is but one example of such sacrifice:

> You, Earth People of the Two-legged Clan, are of all five races, and yet among you there is no understanding of survival. Now that our world has become harsh and barren, it is up to each of you to use your gifts of intuition and creativity in order to survive. Still you will be missing the animal instinct, which would teach you how to recognize danger, find food supplies, know the healing plants, or hear nature's teachers. I offer my body as food for you so that through my body you will gain these instincts. I offer my hide and fur to warm your frail frames. My bones will make tools to aid your survival, and my horns can be fashioned into strong implements to allow you to hunt further. The sinew of my tendons will be thread to sew your clothing, and my hooves will make glue if boiled in my belly with water. This is my gift. Others of the Creature People have agreed that you are in need of what we can offer. Honor our

lives, our instinct, our bodies, and do not waste these gifts. Act now and you will survive.[39]

We are prodigal children—wasteful, extravagant, and imprudent in our treatment of Nature; and oblivious to the natural wildness in us that we inherited from Her. Let us humbly and reverently enter the veld, and coax Her into that field of reunion. And there, let the wild and the tame, and the ground upon which they meet, be re-membered and redeemed.

Reflect

1. Where is your veld? Is it a physical place outdoors, or a spiritual place in your sub- or super-conscious?
2. How do you honor your veld? What ceremonies, rituals, or acts of reverence do you perform there?
3. Are you afraid of dirt? What does "clean" mean to you? (HINT: How many cleaners do you have in your household?)
4. Are there certain wild creatures (as opposed to domesticated ones) that you feel an affinity toward? What meaning do you make of that?

Practice

1. Go outdoors as often as possible.
2. Go barefoot.
3. Play in the dirt.
4. Take walks, or at least sit, in nature. Turn off all electronic devices, and pay attention to the sounds, sights, smells, and textures of nature.
5. Establish or regularly visit a veld space, and nurture it. Talk to the wildlife there, sing to it, thank it, bless it, etc.

6. Research the spirit medicine of the insects, birds, animals, and fish that appear to you while you're out in the veld or wild areas. Ted Andrews' book *Animal Speak* is a great start.
7. Celebrate your successful practice.
8. Repeat as needed.

13

SHED

Boredom, anger, sadness, and fear are not 'yours,' not personal.
They are conditions of the human mind. They come and go.
Nothing that comes and goes is you.

–Eckhart Tolle

The verb "to shed" is most commonly associated with animals who shed what they no longer need, what they grow out of: fur, feathers, skin, exoskeletons, etc. As for humans, perhaps the most familiar use of this verb is associated with weight loss, i.e., "to shed pounds." The difficulty and demands of losing weight are well known, and failure is more common than success, even though the payoff is life-changing.

The etymology of "shed" bears this out. The Old English and Old Germanic meanings of shed include, "to divide, separate, part company; discriminate, decide; scatter abroad, cast off/about." It is believed that these all originate from the PIE root *skei-*, "to cut, separate, divide, part, split."

The first half of the word "schizophrenic" comes from this same root. Original meanings of *schizo-* include "to split, cleave, part, separate;" and also "to shit, to vomit or spit, to break open." More figurative meanings include "to discriminate, to decide" and "distinction, discretion, understanding, reason." The second half of the word, -phrenia, pertains to "mind," and also to the diaphragm, the muscle located in the thorax that makes respiration possible. It originates from the Greek word *phrenos*, "the mind, spirit;" "the midriff, diaphragm;" "parts around the heart, the breast;" and "mind, seat of thoughts."

The practice of shedding asks us to split, as the root word of schizophrenia suggests, so we can experience to some degree two minds simultaneously. Another way of saying it is "to have a foot in both worlds"—one foot in our overweight world while the other steps into the lightweight world. If done effectively, this cleaved state is a temporary one that moves us from one place into another. Not to be confused with the mental illness schizophrenia, this practice of two minds and two places for a brief time heightens our self-awareness. This shedding practice makes us lighter in density and brilliance, and is part of getting in shape for ascension.

Shedding is an initiating process, one that is familiar to our indigenous souls. Initiation, etymologically speaking, means "to go into, enter upon, begin." Our ancestors incorporated initiation rituals into their communal lives in order to move people along in their maturation, growth, and developmental stages. The most significant initiation ceremonies surrounded the transition from childhood to adulthood during puberty rites.

Through the enactment of these practices, candidates shed their childhood, stepping out of their youth into young adulthood. They let go of all that served them well as children, which would only be obstacles on their path to adulthood. This lightened them up in order to inherit what they would need to mature into fully human adults. All initiation rituals are critical to keeping the world going, through what Prechtel calls "the remaking of all things,"[40] perpetually renewing life by releasing to die that which is no longer needed.

Using the weight-loss analogy, our indigenous souls long for us to enter into our internal refrigerators that preserve all of our beliefs and attitudes, and distinguish the ones that are still good for us from the ones that are not. What are we carrying within us that is no longer helping us learn, remember, dream, inter-depend, plant, and all the practices that this book promotes? What have we held onto beyond their expiration date, which hold us back from our own ascension into our higher selves? Let's pull the trashcan over, open the refrigerator door, and discard the following items that diminish us and prevent us from living fully and harmoniously with all of life:

- **Fear** – This probably takes up a whole shelf by itself! Fear is the heaviest and most soul-crushing force that we unnecessarily carry. Consider what the motivation is for most of our actions from day to day—are they fueled more by feelings of uncertainty? The economic, political, religious, and social institutions of our modern Western culture thrive on and perpetuate fear. But if we step away from fear just enough to look at it head on, we can begin to see its illusory effects. Yes, fear is a biological instinct that serves us well. But there is nothing life-giving about chronic fear. We can't outrun it. It drains us, numbs us, separates us and makes us suspicious of each other, and slowly murders us. The new age we are entering into doesn't accommodate fear-based living, so we'll need to do some serious shedding here.

- **Anger** – This sibling of fear is equally effective in separating us from one another, and trapping us in the illusion that we are in competition with one another for whatever is needed to live a happy, healthy life. Also like fear, anger is effective only if we treat it as a lesson from which to learn, not a state in which we remain. We have the choice—we can become students of our anger, or victims of it. We can let anger move us toward resolution and reconciliation, or we can continue to let it gain weight and obstruct our maturation. Our indigenous souls know the importance of diverting the energy we spend on staying angry to resolving whatever conflict threatens the relationships we have or could have with all other forms of life.

- **Judgment and blame** – Nothing works faster to separate us from one another than judging and blaming. The irony is that when we attempt to elevate ourselves over someone by judging or blaming them, we actually drag ourselves down as well. The truth, which our indigenous souls know well, is that every form of life is a mirror, reflecting all other forms of life. Therefore, whenever we judge and blame, we are unconsciously reacting to something we don't like about ourselves. If you've ever been warned not to point accusingly at someone because it meant three fingers were pointing back at you, this is what is happening. Because diminishing one ends up diminishing all, judging and blaming must be shed.

- **Guilt and shame** – These are similar to judge and blame, except the target is often oneself rather than others. Where judging and blaming are often directed toward others, guilt and shame are what we carry in ourselves. While someone else may have inflicted them upon us, we have erroneously agreed to bear them. Yet, as with all the other shed–ables in this chapter, it is perfectly appropriate to utilize the situations that cause shame and guilt as opportunities for learning, as long as we are willing to let go of the shame and guilt once the lesson is learned. Therefore, the reverse of the judge and blame statement is also true: To whatever degree we diminish ourselves we also diminish others.

- **Illusion** – "What is *really* going on here?" is a question that our indigenous souls want us to ask sincerely and frequently. In our everyday occurrences, what is real, and what is illusion? That is our ongoing homework in Earth School. A quote by Phaedrus says it well: "Things are not always what they seem; the first appearance deceives many; the intelligence of a few

71

perceives what has been carefully hidden." With our lives anchored primarily in the 3rd Dimension, we are limited in distinguishing between what is real and what is illusion. For example, what appear to us as opposites (e.g., good vs. bad; dark vs. light; rich vs. poor, birth vs. death) are actually in yin-yang relationships, two sides of the same coin. Another example of illusion that is prominent and perpetuated is that of separation. In the Western culture, the premium placed on independence and self-reliance keeps the illusion of separation alive and well. In reality, everything in existence is reliant on everything else, because of the interconnected web of life that contains us all. Generally speaking, then, we need to shed our convictions that things are indeed as they appear, and be open to new ways of perceiving reality.

- **Expectations** – Attempts to put parameters on things outside of our control is not only futile and maddening, it's restricting. Joseph Rael describes the benefit of shedding our own expectations, to make room for the unexpected: "When the unexpected happens, that is when something new can come in. The unexpected always brings wonderful gifts that we never thought could happen, giving us a whole new idea about the way things really are."[41] Unless we are dealing with things about ourselves, over which we have the most control, our expectations for particular outcomes more often than not lead to disappointment. Many seen and unseen forces influence outcomes, so we are called to devote our energies to putting our best selves into the situation, to offer a prayer for a result that generates the most good to the most people, and to welcome the result whole heartedly.

- **Drama** – In short, this means that we shouldn't let our emotions get out of control to the point that they undermine any growth potential for anyone involved.

- **Karma** – This is an Eastern concept that guarantees that if we have not yet sufficiently learned the lessons we came to the school of Earth to learn, we will reincarnate again and again until we have learned all of our lessons. The Western version of this is "what goes around, comes around." Either way, in order to ascend into a higher dimension of living, all karmic lessons must be completed. When we agree to shedding things we no longer need, we are essentially confirming that we've learned those lessons. The more lessons learned, the fewer trips around the Karmic Wheel we have to take.

Looking back at the etymology of shed and schizophrenia, we see that the heart, lungs, mind, and spirit are all involved. It takes courage and love (heart), discernment (mind), and inspiration (lungs, spirit) to delve deeply into ourselves. It requires an intentional process of raising from our below-the-belt chakras into our above-the-belt chakras each and every encounter we have in life, especially the ones that tempt us to hang onto our shed-ables. Initiation is not for sissies, for it requires the death of our exclusive *self*-focus, so that our *we*-focus can lead us. Only our indigenous souls can take us there.

In summary, shedding provides many benefits. It liberates us from any freeloading, parasitic burdens we carry; it allows for and honors all of the interrelationships in our existence; and it makes us more energy efficient because our load is lighter AND we have others to help us carry. Shedding initiates us into a new way of being that allows us to understand how connected we are to everything. What we lose in shedding, we more than gain in realizing our capacity to be fully human.

In this new age, we are called to cast off that which no longer works, that which is no longer sustainable, that which no longer serves a high purpose. In this unprecedented time, we must become literally and figuratively lighter, in order to ascend to higher Dimensions of consciousness. The etymology of shed indicates that much patience-soaked discretion, understanding, and reason is required in order for us to distinguish between what is and what is not useful anymore. The next chapter offers a related practice to help us with some very specialized shedding.

Reflect

1. Reflect on the times in your life when you tried to shed that which was no longer useful to you. Were you successful? Why or why not?
2. Which of the recommended shed-able items listed in this chapter are of highest priority for you, and why? What is absent from this list that is high on your own personal list?
3. The literal meaning of "initiate" is "to go in." Are you willing to delve inside of yourself to discern what you need to shed from your life?

Practice

1. Create and prioritize your own personal list of shed-ables, which may or may not include the ones recommended in this chapter.
2. For each item on your own list, spell out specific strategies that will help you shed it from your life.
3. Prepare yourself accordingly for the void that remains whenever you successfully shed. With what will you fill the void? How will your relationships change as you shed?
4. Review Chapter 11 ("Feel") as needed, to assist you in the process of vibrating at a higher energetic level (i.e., elevating the situation from your lower chakras to your higher ones). Just as exercising at a high level helps to shed physical pounds, spiritually vibrating at a high level helps to shed psychological pounds.

5. Refer to the next chapter ("Forgive") and consider this very specialized skill in shedding.
6. Celebrate your successful practice.
7. Repeat as needed.

14

FORGIVE

Before you embark on a journey of revenge, dig two graves.

−Confucius

Forgiveness is perhaps the most difficult, and consequently the most redemptive form of shedding that we can practice. Two widely known sayings about forgiveness are "Forgive us our debts as we forgive our debtors," and "Forgive and forget." The common etymology of "forgive," "forget," and "debt" is surprising.

"Forgive" comes from the Old English word *forgiefan*, "give, grant, allow; remit (a debt), pardon (an offense)." *For-* comes from the PIE root **pr-*, meaning "forward, through;" and has extended meanings including "in front of, before, first, toward, at, near, around, about." *-Give*, from the Old English word *giefan* ("bestow, deliver to another, grant, pardon, allot, devote, entrust"), comes from the PIE root **ghabh-*, "to take, hold, have, give." "Habit" comes from this same PIE root, and means "to hold," but it can be used to mean either "offer" or "take."

"Forget" is from the Old English word *forgietan* (note the near-identical spelling to the Old English word for "forgive"), which means "lose the power of recalling to mind, fail to remember, neglect inadvertently." Forget is made up of *for-* and *-get,* which comes from the PIE roots **ghend-* and **ghed-,* both meaning, "to seize or take."

"Debt" actually comes from the combination of *de-* ("away, down from, off, undo"), and *habere* ("to have"), which is closely related to "habit," sharing the same PIE root **ghabh-.*

In summary, consider these interpretations:

- To forgive and forget is to pardon the unresolved give-and-take relationships we have with others, and then move forward. It is to hold out our hands in reconciliatory offering and pardon, and then to carry on without grudge.

- To ask for our debts to be forgiven is to ask for pardon for our unresolved give-and-take relationships.

- Similarly, to forgive our debtors is to grant pardon for our unresolved give-and-take relationship with them.

- Alternatively, to ask for forgiveness of our debts as we forgive our debtors is to seek pardon from our mistakes and faults that have burdened others; and to return that freeing favor.

Neil Douglas-Klotz presents a perspective that offers forgiveness as an option for filling the void that remains after the shedding process. In his translation and commentary on the Lord's Prayer, he writes:

> Besides "forgive," the roots of the [Aramaic] word *washboqlan* may also be translated "return to its original state," "reciprocally absorb," "reestablish slender ties to," and "embrace with emptiness." The prayer reaffirms that our original state is clear and unburdened, one where our slender ties to creation are based on mutual releasing, with every breath we breathe.[42]

These two statements provide a wealth of information about forgiveness. The first line reveals how utterly restorative forgiveness is to our relationships with one another. Additionally, reciprocity is built right into the act of forgiveness, asking each party to "absorb" the originally intact relationship into themselves. This demands much of us, as does the criterion of "embracing with emptiness," obliging us to re-enter the relationship without agendas and to depart without grudges. Douglas-Klotz also identifies another critical component of forgiveness: the necessity of repetition and consistency—"with every breath we breathe."

It is also worth adding the importance of self-forgiveness, which is often the hardest to render. Right relationship with anyone or anything else is dependent upon right relationship with oneself. The Law of One, which is described in the next chapter, explains and supports this statement more fully.

Shedding and forgiving lighten our loads, accelerate our vibration levels, restore us to our whole minds and whole selves, and prepare us well for higher consciousness and awareness. The next step is to restock our cleaned-out refrigerators with life-giving food that nourishes our indigenous souls.

Reflect

1. Reflect on a situation in your life in which you forgave someone, or someone forgave you. How were you changed by the experience?
2. Now reflect on a missed opportunity for you to offer or receive forgiveness. Do you have regrets about it? Is it too late to reconcile the relationship now?
3. What things have you forgiven yourself for? What things await self-forgiveness?

Practice

1. Retroactively forgive. Make a list of people that you have not forgiven for something they did or said that hurt or offended you. Give due consideration to each person on your list, and establish a plan for reconciling your relationship with each one of them.
2. Proactively forgive. From now on and with every breath:
   - Free others with your pardon.
   - Recover and nurture your relationships.
   - Release agendas and grudges.
3. Ask for forgiveness, from others and from yourself.
4. Celebrate your successful practice.
5. Repeat as needed.

15

YIELD

Strength is found in those who let go of how it is 'supposed'
to happen, who yield to the process that gives life
to the next generations.

–Jamie Sams

What does a "YIELD" sign at an intersection ask of us? It warns us that traffic coming from other directions has the right-of-way, and so we need to slow down enough to make sure our path is clear of oncoming traffic before we proceed. More specifically, it tells us to give up or pay forward the right to go first. The verb "yield" comes from the PIE root *gheldh-*, which means, "to pay." Old English, Proto-Germanic, and Old Norse words from this root mean, "to pay for, reward, render; worship, serve, sacrifice to; repay, return; to cost, be worth." The definition of "give up, submit, surrender as to a foe" is a later interpretation.

In a previous chapter, we were invited to shed what is no longer useful, and this creates room for something that serves the greater good, which includes us. In this chapter, we are encouraged to yield to that which replaces what we've shed, acknowledging that its power is greater than ours, and its rewards exceed what we let go of. Further, we are asked to yield in a respectful, honorable way that recognizes the worthiness of what we're yielding to.

In this regard, yielding is an act of reverence. Granted, few of us see traffic signs as worthy of our *reverence*, but we certainly see them as worthy of our *respect*, and so we abide by them. Traffic signs are a function of human-made laws to exert control and maintain order. However, the shedding that was prescribed earlier was to yield not to human-made laws, but to Cosmic Law. There's a big difference.

Cosmic (or Divine) Law can also be thought of as the collective laws of nature, which describe how the universe works. An underlying truth of Cosmic Law is that everything in the universe—seen and unseen—is alive, and each is a component of the whole living entity. This truth further recognizes that the whole has the capacity to sustain, adapt, and perpetuate itself.

While Cosmic Law is as old as the universe itself, the recording and teaching of its laws originated thousands of years ago, most notably in the ancient Greek, Egyptian, and Vedic (Indian) cultures. Esoteric writings and teachings of various world religions also reflect an acknowledgement of and reverence for these natural laws.

How do Cosmic Law and Human Law compare? Human-made laws are created and imposed to accomplish what someone *wants* the order of things to be. In contrast, Cosmic Law describes how something *is*, naturally. Human-made laws can and will change to reflect the times, circumstances, and preferences of the people; but Cosmic Law is immune to these forces.

Fluctuations in human-made laws have no bearing on Cosmic Law, because Cosmic Law explains how things work in the universe regardless of what human beings do. Where human-made law says, "We need to *do it this* way;" Cosmic Law says, "It *is this* way. It is what it is!" The more synchronization there is between any human-made law and Cosmic Law, the longer the human-made law will endure and the greater the well-being of all of Creation.

You may be more familiar with how cosmic laws work in your life than you realize. There are many familiar sayings and quotable quotes that reflect how nature works in our lives, such as:

- "This too shall pass."
- "The more things change, the more they stay the same."
- "Necessity is the mother of invention."
- "Seek and ye shall find. Knock and the door will be opened to you."
- "When a door closes, a window opens."
- "The more I learn, the less I know."

If any of these ring true for you, you are an adherent of cosmic laws.

How many cosmic laws are there? It varies, depending on the information source. Some sources say as few as seven, while others identify hundreds. The highest number I've seen so far in my research is 492! Here are eight that I have found most helpful in reviving my indigenous soul:

- **Law of One** – All is One. Everything that exists comprises the One, the infinite Creator (also called other names, including "God"). There is no separation (any appearance of separation is an illusion) or opposites, and thus no judgment or competition, because that would mean the One is in conflict with itself. All is love and light. Every entity is perfect in its completeness. This law reminds me that I am in unity with not only all that I love and find desirable, but also all that I find hard to love or find desirable. I can't pick and choose who or what I'm bound to in the Universe. The "good" and the "bad" are united.

- **Law of Vibration** – Everything that is created is energetic in form. As such, everything vibrates. Vibrations that are sent out for the greater good (e.g., prayer, gratitude) are at a higher frequency and return the gift of higher Dimensions of consciousness. Vibrations that are sent out for selfish purposes (e.g. greed, power over, envy) are at a lower frequency and impose limitations on consciousness. This law validates and encourages the prayers and meditations that I send out for the good of all creation, knowing that they benefit me as much as the addressees.

- **Law of Free Will** – Every entity created has the right to direct its own life and pursue its own quality of life as long as it doesn't infringe upon the free will of other entities. Even the unseen powers must abide by this law – the spirit world stands ready and anxious to accompany, guide, and assist us, but we must ask for this help. Spirit cannot impose upon our lives unless we call upon it, no matter what. The *only* and *extremely rare* exception to this rule is if the entire planet is in danger of complete destruction. This law has released me from the self-imposed responsibility of helping people run their own lives!

- **Law of Do No Harm** – This important corollary to the Law of Free Will says that the only limitation on one's free will is when it intentionally or potentially causes harm. I once heard it stated this way: "The freedom that you have to swing your fist stops at the point where it reaches my nose." This law helps me consider the ramifications of my decisions on other people's lives and free will.

- **Law of Attraction** –You attract what you are. What you think and exude, you draw to you. The more consistent and repetitious your thoughts are, the more you will attract to you what you are thinking. To think is to manifest into being. This law reminds me that my thoughts, feelings, and actions are energetic magnets, and that I have the power to affect which people and situations appear in my life. It also reminds me that any negative or fear-based energies I exude will only draw more negativity and fear, and likewise positive and love-based energies will attract positive and loving people and situations.

- **Law of Allowing or Law of Manifestation** – An important complement to the Law of Attraction, this Law essentially says that the manifestor of thoughts must believe in what he is thinking, and must believe that the Universe will provide all that is needed for his growth. Further, the manifestor must believe that he is worthy of and has the right to receive from the Universe without guilt or judgment, at the energy cost that he thinks is fair (i.e., what he is willing to gift back to the Universe in return). This law reveals that I have more power to create my reality than I realize, and that I am worthy of and capable of using my power to do so. This law helps me move beyond lip-service, to act upon my firm belief that I can and do create my own reality.

- **Law of Change** — The essence of this law can be summarized in these two familiar statements: "The only thing we can be certain of is change," and "This, too, shall pass." African shaman Malidoma Some´ informs us of the distinction between Spirit-induced change and human-induced change: "In the indigenous context, change is tolerated, even welcomed, because it originates with Spirit. If evolution originates in a spiritual source, then it does not disrupt stability. If it is concerned with ascendency, acquisition, and control and mastery over the material world, then evolution becomes destructive to stability."[43] Either way, the Law of Change still applies. This law helps me stay on my toes, regarding change. It helps me loosen the grip on any expectations I have, and it makes me stay mentally, emotionally, and spiritually flexible.

- **Law of Chaos and Law of Order** – Of help to us in times of change, these two laws indicate that "chaos" and "order" are in the eyes of the beholder: Chaos is the state in which the observer *cannot* accept what is; and Order is the state in which the observer *can* accept what is, even if things seem to be chaotic. This law helps me to be open to different interpretations of any given situation or stimulus. It also reminds me to trust that the universe knows what it's doing even when I don't know what it's doing, and sometimes when I don't know what *I'm* doing!

What a gift it is to have these Cosmic Laws available to us, to help us navigate our way in this multi-dimensional universe we live in! To decline the invitation to this information, deferring to our human-made laws, would be like trying to play a basketball game on a football field. To resist Cosmic Law is to threaten the quality and quantity of all of life, and to defy cosmic wisdom.

Cosmic Law is a healthy substitute for what we shed to prepare for our ascension into higher Dimensions of existence and awareness. Our indigenous souls know that we embody these laws, as the universe that surrounds us is also within us. Now is the time to return to ("come back" to), and sacrifice ("sacredly perform") and serve ("render habitual obedience to") in accordance with these Laws of the Universe.

Reflect

1. You've heard or even used the common response, "That's just not natural!" What does this statement mean to you when you say it or hear it?
2. Have you ever said, in response to a situation that appears to be out of your control, "Well, God is in charge," or "The universe knows what it's doing," or something similar?
    *   What did you mean by your statement?
    *   Did your yielding cause you to become frustrated? Or did it bring you relief?

3. Reflect on a time where you questioned the logic or wisdom of a human-made rule, policy or law.
    • What was the purpose of the policy?
    • What made you think it wasn't going to work or wasn't necessary?
    • Did it conflict with Cosmic Law?

Practice

1. Conduct an internet search on "Cosmic Law" and see how many variations there are.
    • Which sources seem to be most helpful to you, and why?
    • What common sayings are you familiar with that reflect some of these Cosmic Laws? (e.g., "It's always darkest before dawn," or "Whether you believe it not, you're right.")
2. In your daily routines, look for examples of Human Law compared to Universal Law.
    • When are they compatible?
    • When do they conflict?
3. Pick one or two of the Cosmic Laws that you want to focus on for yourself, and practice conforming to them until you find yourself defaulting to them easily and naturally. Then pick two more.
4. Celebrate your successful practice.
5. Repeat as needed.

16

LOVE

One teacha dat teach God's Rules wen stand up fo aks Jesus one question fo trick him. He say, "Teacha, wat I gotta do fo get da real kine life dat stay to da max foeva?" Jesus say, "Get love an aloha fo da Boss yoa God wit all yoa heart, and wit everyting inside you, an wit how you tink, and wit all yoa power. An get love an aloha fo everybody jalike you get love fo yoaself." Jesus say, "Dass right! Do dat an you goin live fo real kine."

–Luke 10:25-28, *Da Jesus Book* (Hawaii Pidgin New Testament)

Translation: *Just then a lawyer stood up to test Jesus. "Teacher, what must I do to inherit eternal life?" Jesus said, "You shall love the Lord your God with all your heart, and with all your soul, and with all your strength, and with all your mind; and your neighbor as yourself. Do this and you will live."*

–Bible, New Revised Standard Version

Practice-wise, we've come to the midpoint of the book, and not coincidentally we now explore the heart of the entire cosmic and indigenous matter—love. Jesus is featured prominently in this chapter for several reasons, the first being the centrality of love in his ministry. The opening quote is just one of several Bible passages in which Jesus identifies love as the greatest commandment.

Secondly, Jesus has historically and internationally been viewed as the very embodiment and expression of love. "Jesus loves me, this I know" is just one of many well-known songs and affirmations that demonstrate the influence of Jesus' message of love.

Finally, a key aspect of love that is also central in Jesus' ministry is the indigenous nature of love. Remember that "indigenous" means "in-born." In the above passage, Jesus clearly identifies the planes of our bodies that cooperate perfectly to carry out the greatest commandment: heart (emotional), soul (spiritual), strength (physical), and mind (mental). Jesus wouldn't prioritize love if he thought we weren't capable of it. In fact, we're wired for it!

The word "love" comes from the Old English word *lufian*, which means, "cherish, delight in, approve, show love to or feel love for." It comes from the PIE root *leubh-*, which means, "to care, desire, love." Other meanings include "please, dear, beloved, affection, friendliness, and love of God." "Heart," the organ primarily but not exclusively associated with love, comes from the Old English word *heorte*, referring not only to the muscle which is responsible for circulating blood, but also referring to "breast, soul, spirit, will, desire, courage, mind, and intellect." "Heart" comes from the PIE root *kerd-* ("heart"), the same root of similar Old European words that mean "middle."

The etymology of these two terms indicates that love is at the center, the middle, and it radiates through our whole being. The biblical passage at the beginning of the chapter indicates that it is also at the center of how to live our lives.

What kind of love are we to practice? In John 15:9-12, Jesus names two qualities in particular: abiding and agape. In the Greek language, the original language of the New Testament, abide is *meno*, which literally means "stay, live, dwell, or lodge." Other translations of this Greek word are "enduring, lasting, surviving, and permanent." Just through these translations, we get a sense that this is no ordinary love.

Loosely translated, "abide in my love" means "Hang out here in this kind of love. Hole up in this kind of love, bathe in it, wear it, breathe it, cream your coffee with it and drizzle it over your pancakes, build your house on it, raise your families in it, rest your head on it, go to sleep by it, wake up with it and do it all again, every day." *That's* the kind of love that Jesus asks us to share with one another, because he knows from experience how awesome it is.

Agape is the Greek word for love, and in particular, it refers to love that is God-like. So when Jesus commands us to love one another as God loves us, he means: "Be God-like in your love for one another. Put your BIG LOVE pants on and give it all you've got. Give the kind of love that persists, endures, welcomes, forgives, uplifts, companions, heals, and frees."

What does abiding, agape love look like? How are we to love? Let us count some of the ways:

1. Completely, with everything we've got and all that we are, with all our hearts and souls;
2. Courageously, because "for heaven to begin, love has to manifest in hell;"[44]
3. Constantly, in each moment of our lives, letting "What would LOVE do?" be our guiding mantra;
4. Kindly, with rose-colored glasses that allow us to see the divine nature in everything and everyone, even if their behavior is unbecoming;
5. Confidently, because love is the birthplace of miracles; and
6. Naturally, because love is who we are and what we know instinctively from the time we are born.

Who are we to love? God and others, as the scripture says. But we are also called to love our enemies—a difficult task. And, we are called to love ourselves—for some reason, an even more difficult task.

According to the Law of One, if we love others, friend or foe, then we love ourselves, too. Conversely if we truly love ourselves, then we will find it easy to love others who don't appear to be lovable. We will be able to see past the unlovable parts about them, because we've been able to see past the unlovable parts about ourselves. Further, when we forgive ourselves for our unlovable parts, we concurrently forgive others for their unlovable parts. Because All is One, love and forgiveness for one means ALL are loved and forgiven.

In the New Testament passages where Jesus tells us to love our enemies, the Greek word for "enemy" is *echthra,* and this word also means "hostility" and "hatred."[45] A different Greek word meaning "enemy" is *polemioi* (from *polemeo*), which means, "one who fights, battles, attacks, makes war."[46] Notice the different meanings of the two different Greek words that are both translated as "enemy;" and notice that Jesus used the lesser of the two extremes. The etymology of "enemy" reveals that it comes from *in-* ("not") + *amicus/amare* ("friend/to love'), and basically it means, "an unfriend." Perhaps Jesus is emphasizing that those we perceive as being hostile or hateful to us are merely folks we haven't made friends with yet. Here's where our courage to love is called upon. When we convert "unfriends" to friends, fights and attacks will cease. When we practice love in the face of hatred and hostility, war will be no more.

Why is love the greatest commandment? Because love is the pathway to personal, communal, and planetary ascension, and that pathway runs through our hearts. "Does this path have a heart?" Carlos Castaneda asks us. "If it does, the path is good. If it doesn't, it is of no use. One makes for a joyful journey, the other will make you curse your life."[47] In this life as in all of our previous lives; in this 3rd Dimension as in all the Dimensions of our multi-dimensional selves; and in this cosmic time of planetary shift, love is the path.

Furthermore, it's the law, a commandment. There is a Universal Law of Love, which has two very important parts.

First, it places the concern for others above oneself. In the context of All is One, we recognize that there is no separation between self and others, because both are All. "All" means there's no "other." So when we love to the extent that we prioritize the welfare of others, we're actually acknowledging and loving ALL, which includes ourselves.

Second, the Universal Law of Love indicates that we are not to resist evil (except when our safety is threatened! In that case, it is appropriate to resist the harm that we are threatened with.) "Resist" literally means, "to firmly stand against" or "oppose," and this is incompatible with the Law of One—we would be opposing ourselves! Love instead transforms evil by exposing the illusion of separation that it thrives on, and substituting the reality of All is One. It all comes down to algebra (from the Arabic words *al ajbr*—"reunion of broken parts;" and *jabara*—"reintegrate, reunite, consolidate").

Follow closely:

1. If love is our natural state, then we are love.
2. If All is One, then we are All.
3. If we are Love (from #1), and we are All (from #2), then Love is All.
4. Therefore, Love is all there is. Love is the only thing that's real. And *that's* the heart of the matter.

Reflect

1. Who is easy for you to love, and why? Who is hard for you to love, and why?
2. Do you have any "enemies?" How do you love them?
3. Which is easier for you to love: others, or yourself? Why do you think this is true for you?

Practice

1. Craft your own "Greatest Commandment" that expresses your own beliefs about love. Does it include yourself, others, and God? Who else, or who instead?

2. The word "Aloha" is a very important word in the quote at the beginning of the chapter. Beyond "hello" and "goodbye," what does "Aloha" really mean? Research the deeper meaning of this word.

3. Look up synonyms of the word "love." Do they reflect the abiding and agape characteristics of the kind of love that Jesus asks of us?

4. Look up the etymology of the word "hate." Is there any indication of this word being the opposite of love? How does the etymology support (or not) Jesus' commandment to love our enemies?

5. How do *you* love? In addition to the counted ways listed in the chapter, count the ways that *you* love.

6. Celebrate your successful practice.

7. Repeat as needed.

17

RESPOND

Every person is sent to this outpost called Earth to work on a project
that is intended to keep the cosmic order healthy. Any person that fails
to do what he or she must do energetically stains the cosmic order.

–Malidoma Some´

In the book, *The Orenda*, a scene takes place in 17th century Canada, around a conversation between a Huron Indian chief and a visiting French Jesuit priest. The two men are preparing for a canoe trip that they'll take together the following day through some difficult and dangerous territory.

The chief refers to the pristine wilderness the Natives call home and asks, "Do you like this place?"

The priest answers, "Yes, I do."

The chief thinks for a moment and then says to the priest in dead seriousness: "Tomorrow, you must make the decision either to paddle or not to paddle. You will be respected only if you make a firm choice. You can't choose in the middle. Paddle or don't paddle. If you don't paddle, then maybe tell those in your canoe a story about your god. If you do paddle, don't talk, just paddle. Paddle until the rest of us stop paddling. There is no middle out here."[48]

This chapter is about paddling, as opposed to riding along. It's about responding rather than reacting. "Respond" comes from the Latin word *respondere*, meaning "answer to, promise in return." It is composed of *re-* ("back to the original place; again, anew, once more; against"), and *–spond*, from the Latin *spondere* ("to pledge"). This second half of the word comes from the Greek word *spondeios*, which is "the name of the meter originally used in chants accompanying libations," and refers literally to a drink offering. It comes from the PIE root *spend-*, which means "to make an offering, perform a rite; engage oneself by a ritual act."

"React" has the same prefix (*re-*), followed by *act*, which comes from the PIE root *ag-*, meaning, "to drive, draw out or forth, to move; to do, perform." The contrast between these two words obviously comes from their second syllables. While responding involves a relationship of deep reverence, reacting implies a solitary movement that doesn't necessarily include any sort of reflection, let alone a relationship. Compared to the worship-like nature of "respond," "react" is merely reflex, moving in an ingrained, familiar way without giving it much thought.

When we choose to respond instead of react, we agree to engage ourselves, to make an offering of ourselves in the form of a promise, a commitment of ourselves to something or someone. To respond is to take the experience that we encounter, such as an action, a spoken message or an event, and carry it to the altar of discernment. At this altar we and the experience commune. We sit on the same ground, breathe each other's air, and entertain each other's meaning. Only after that ritual do we *act*, not *re-act*. And we act in a manner that is worthy of the exchange at the altar. When we let the altar experience inform how we act and speak, then our actions and words are *responses*, not *reactions*.

The short dialogue between the Huron chief and the Jesuit priest brings them both to the altar of discernment. The question the chief asks the priest is not a casual one at all, but rather a soul-searching one. This story takes place during the time of the infiltration of Christian missionaries into the First Nations' land and culture. Their goal was to convert North American Indians to Christianity, thereby "saving" them from their savage and primitive ways. While this chief and his people are generally welcoming to the Jesuits, they remain cautious and alert to the Jesuits' mission to undermine their very way of life. Thus, the chief's question invites the priest to join him at the altar of discernment.

Now it's the priest's turn. Both he and the chief know that "Do you like this place?" does not mean, "Are you enjoying yourself?" It means, "Can you see the value of this place and our people enough to let it all be?" Hopefully the priest honored such a question with some altar time before responding, "Yes, I do."

While still at the altar, the chief takes the priest at his word, and then explains the rules of responsiveness and responsibility: paddle, or talk; don't do both, and don't do neither. As they leave the altar to enter the canoe, each has discerned his own responsibility: The chief is to honor the priest's participation in the canoe, and the priest is to honor the Native Americans, their land, and their ways.

The altar of discernment is within us, in our upper chakras. The notable distinction between *emote* and *feel* is similar to that between *react* and *respond*: Emoting and reacting are tied up in the chakras below the belt, and feeling and responding are above-the-belt actions.

The saying, "take it to heart" captures exactly what the essence of responding is—it is taking what we experience, holding it close to our hearts and minds, letting it be a part of us and letting it change us, and honoring it by saying a toast to it. To respond is to treat a stimulus as a gift, and to commend oneself to it. To react, on the other hand, is to treat a stimulus as an obstacle or potential threat, and to deflect it. Responding is a ritual act, inviting us to make ceremony of our daily interactions. Our indigenous souls are naturally inclined to do so, and our bodies are perfectly hard-wired for it.

How are we to be *responsible* ("answerable, accountable") and *responsive* ("making an answer") adults? As unique individuals, we are responsible *for* our own thoughts, words, and deeds. As interdependent individuals, we are responsible *to* others by being accountable for all we do and say; and by holding others equally accountable for their own actions and words.

We are responsive through our thoughts, words, and deeds. In an earlier chapter our thoughts, words, and actions were likened to seeds. Responding is like sowing seeds, so we must be ever aware that everything we think, say, and do puts energy into motion. Our thought processes initiate that whole sequence, so mindfulness is what is needed. Our hearts and minds are partners in the discernment process, and in directing the body toward spoken and active response.

Listening is the necessary precursor to responsive speech. Without listening, there would be nothing to carry to the altar, and speaking would be mere reaction. Jamie Sams tells us, "When people are constantly talking about anything that comes to their minds, it is a sign that they have no self-reflective skills and do not feel the weight or sacredness that their words carry. If the words that are spoken carry no commitment or carelessly hurt another, the speaker is not in tune with Oneness."[49]

Knowing the importance of listening, our ancestors used the Talking Stick method of conversation, whereby only the person who held the stick was allowed to speak without interruption, and everyone else had to listen intently. Every person was granted a turn with the stick, and every person was responsible for listening carefully to what others said during their allotted turns.

In our current age of rapid, one-way, and often faceless communication through our electronic devices, the Talking Stick method may appear time-consuming and tedious. But its accomplishments are enviable: each person's contribution was valued; people were responded to, not reacted to; and the occurrence of impertinent information, irrelevant questions, and idle chatter was drastically reduced or eliminated altogether. Additionally, the Talking Stick method included the importance of respecting what each person had to say, even if there was disagreement. Our indigenous souls yearn for the return of this kind of listening-based communication in our daily interactions with one another.

Our speech contains power. However, we often lack awareness of that power. For starters, we speak more than strings of letters. The etymology of any word reveals its unique history, geography, sociology, psychology, and more. The practice employed throughout this book testifies to the truth that words live, and their meanings morph over time and through centuries of use. Our words land on the ears of our ancestors, assuring them that life continues through us, because of our utterances.

In addition to the power of their ancestral lineage, our words also carry energetic power. Picture the ripples on water caused by a tossed pebble. This is what happens in the air when we speak. Each word casts its own unique vibration, and also carries the vibration of the person speaking, thus influencing the whole cosmos. That's why mantras exude power—they combine the physical vibrations of word sounds with the speaker's mindful and heart-full intent. This is also why indigenous ceremony vocalizations repeat. It's not because the Holies have hearing or attention deficit problems; it's because the energies produced are like touches, and repeating the sounds over and over again is like giving the spiritual realm a massage!

Our indigenous souls know that we not only offer our speech, we *are* speech. We exist because we were spoken into being, sung into being, sounded into being. Martin Prechtel explains this Maya perspective:

> Speech is in all things. The nature of grass to grow is the speech of the spirit of grass. The flowering of trees is the speech of a tree's spirit, as is the time of year when they flower. The Gods and their nature in the other worlds of creation don't talk *about* things, like us humans; they talk life into solid moving forms

97

by repeating the sacred names of life over and over. Their words take on form.[50]

Consider these other examples of the creative nature of sound: Ohm, with its specific pronunciation, in the Buddhist and Hindu traditions; Word/Logos in the Judeo/Christian tradition; the heartbeat of Mother Earth speaking through Native American drum beats; and didgeridoo playing by Aborigines to replicate how God created the stars.

Knowing the deep and proud connection that exists between our language and our ancestors, and realizing the creative power of the sounds our voices make, might it be worthwhile to always give pause before we speak?

This book of practices focuses on our responsiveness through action. Performed ritually—repeatedly and reverently—these practices will go a long way in helping us to do our part in keeping the cosmic order healthy. These practices will guide us in fulfilling our unique purposes for being on Earth at this time.

If we want life to continue, we must paddle.

Reflect

1. Reflect on a particular time that you *reacted* instead of *responded* to a situation.
   - What was your objective in reacting the way you did? Was it accomplished?
   - How was the relationship affected between you and the person(s) you reacted to?
   - If you had the chance to re-live that experience, would you change anything? If so, what? And why?
   - What might your *response* look like in this situation, rather than your *reaction*?

2. Reflect on a memorable conversation you had with one or more people that left a lasting impression on you.
   - What happened during that conversation that made it stand out to you? Was it the topic, or the communication process, or both?
   - What was absent, and what was present, that made this conversation different than less-memorable conversations?
   - Based on your answers, how would you distinguish a *responsive* conversation from a *reactive* one?

Practice

1. If you haven't done so already, create an altar of response within yourself.
   - Get quiet, and block out distractions.
   - Closing your eyes helps, especially if you are very new to your inner self.
   - Ask yourself whatever question works to elevate your energies to your above-the-belt chakras (e.g., "What would love do in this situation?" or "What trigger just happened?" or "What's *really* going on here, and what's just drama?")
   - Intuit and embrace the answers you come up with, and rest them in this altar space until you form a response that is satisfactory to your better (i.e., higher vibrating) self.
2. Practice using your altar space as often as possible. There are countless opportunities for its use in any given day of your life. The more you practice, the more efficient you will become: you will need less time to generate a thoughtful response, and you will feel more naturally inclined to bypass the reaction option completely.
3. Revisit the "Feel" chapter if needed, especially the Practice section, to review some strategies that may help you shift from reaction to response.

4. If your reaction slips out before you are able to elevate your energies into response mode, all is not lost. Confess to yourself and the party to whom you reacted that you failed to give yourself time to respond instead of react. Apologize, and ask for an opportunity to replace your reaction with a response.

5. During conversation with others, practice your listening skills as if there really was a Talking Stick being passed among you.

6. Before speaking, remember that what comes out of your mouth is energy that instantly and irretrievably changes the environment outside of your mouth, the moment your words make sound. Therefore, take your time in crafting a *response* for your speech, rather than a *reaction*.

7. Celebrate your successful practice.

8. Repeat as needed.

18

FEED

The planet eats the effort we expend, our prayers, sacred chanting, group worship, or our exertion in physical work. This is what the planet lives on. It is the effort that we place on our daily attempts to reach our highest physical, mental, emotional, and spiritual potential that the planet uses to survive.

–Joseph Rael

Be Fed. Feed. Be the Food. This is the sequence that Chapter 3 introduces, and it's not a bad idea to review that chapter again before proceeding into this chapter. Where Chapter 3 emphasizes the youthful practice of being fed, here we explore the adult practice of feeding. Among other practices, Shed, Yield, Love, and Forgive have prepared us well for what "feed" now asks of us.

In review, "feed" comes from the PIE root *pa-, which means "to tend, keep, pasture, protect, guard, feed." The Old English word *fedan* means "nourish, give food to, sustain, foster." "Nourish" comes from the Old French *norrir* and the Latin word *nutrire*, which mean "raise, bring up, foster, maintain, provide for; support, preserve, nurse." Both come from the PIE root *(s)nau-, meaning "to swim, flow, let flow; to suckle" (i.e., nursing, breast-feeding).

Considering this utterly organic basis of "feed," the final pages of John Steinbeck's novel, *The Grapes of Wrath*, come to mind. In the desperate times of the Dust Bowl and the Great Depression, a young woman goes into labor and delivers her stillborn baby—dead, due to lack of nutrition. Yet the following day she is able to save someone else's life through the most literal translation of "feed" that one can think of.

Although the movie version of the story has a different ending, its script is equally consistent with the etymology of "feed." As the Joad family departs for yet another promise of work, Pa bemoans that things will never be the same again. Ma replies that, from a woman's perspective, the ups and downs and beginnings and endings in life constitute one continuous flow. Both of these endings present the same challenge, "How are we keeping the flow of life going?"

Another movie comes to mind, a childhood favorite of mine. In "Mary Poppins," the "Feed the Birds" song and scene mesmerized and left their permanent imprint on me. What resonated with me then was how animals are our friends, how important it is for us to take care of them, and how adults see the world differently than children do. The question this haunting song posed then—and still does—is, "If *I* don't feed them, who will?"

From an indigenous perspective, everything is alive. "Inanimate" is an oxymoron. The life force within everything can be viewed as spiritual or as energetic—either is an accurate description. From a scientific standpoint, the fact that everything is made up of energy points to the liveliness within everything, even human-made creations. So, if everything is alive, then everything must be fed, in order to stay alive. What food can we offer?

Literally speaking, offering food to those who hunger is the most basic and obvious requirement. Such feeding is a staple of interdependence, indebtedness, and belonging. In the absence of these connections, food is wasted while people go to bed hungry. Mother Earth is more than capable of providing sufficient nourishment for all of her children, so it is up to us to make sure that no one is starving.

Figuratively speaking, feeding is the practice of offering whatever is necessary to nurture someone or something; and what constitutes food is limited only by our passion-driven imaginations. Figuratively speaking, the hungry are those whose vulnerability places them, at least temporarily, at risk: our young, our old, our sick, our troubled, our isolated.

Because feeding is the earliest and most basic function of parenting, the most obvious audience for our practice of feeding is our young. Feeding them includes helping them learn and remember who they are and where they came from. It includes teaching them what we have learned through our initiation experiences, and supporting them through their own. And to the extent that all in the village who hunger benefit, feeding includes being responsible adults who assume leadership that is committed to the good of the whole. Feeding and eldering go hand in hand.

In addition to our human brothers and sisters, other life forms on earth also need to be fed. Gaia is the name given to planet Earth as acknowledgement that She is alive. So even as we rely absolutely and completely upon Her for our very existence and maintenance, She, too, needs to be fed by us. This is especially true as She is ascending into higher Dimensions, healing from the cosmic and human hits She has taken over tens of thousands of years. Just as aging parents and grandparents need some assistance from their offspring, Mother Earth could use ours!

How can we feed the Mother who feeds us? In addition to saying "thank you" with our every breath, we can feed her in three categorical ways: by ceasing our Gaia-maiming ways of living; by replenishing what she has lost through natural and unnatural wear and tear; and by honoring and celebrating Her. Joseph Rael's quote at the beginning of the chapter provides additional guidance, indicating to us that every decision we make about how we live our lives will either feed or starve Mother Earth.

Since our births, we've been fed. Now our charge is to feed, because it's our turn to do so. We feed, because to do so honors those who fed us, and those who fed the ones who fed us, and so on. We feed because we want life to go on, to continue to flow. We must. If we don't feed, who will?

Reflect

1. Reflect on the indigenous understanding that everything is alive. Does this resonate with you completely? Or are there some things that are obviously alive, and other things obviously non-living to you? Where do you draw the line between the two, and why?
2. How do *you* feed the world? In what ways do you keep the flow of life going?

Practice

1. For one week, keep a record of the instances you "feed" (in every sense of the word) something or someone. At the end of the week, evaluate your results:
   • Who and what did you feed?
   • In addition to the obviously-living recipients of your food (e.g., people, animals, plants) were there any not-so-obviously living recipients (e.g., your car, your computer, your home, a street or a bridge)?
   • What "food" did you provide?
   • Did the frequency of your feeding increase over the week, because you paid more attention as the week went on?
2. Re-read the quote at the beginning of this chapter. Now that you've been reminded of all that qualifies as "food," what are some new ways to feed your world that you weren't aware of before? Add them to your repertoire.
3. Celebrate your successful practice.
4. Repeat as needed.

19

STORY

Story is the umbilical cord that connects us to the past, present, and future.
Story is a relationship between the teller and
the listener, a responsibility . . .
an affirmation of our ties to one another.

–Terry Tempest Williams

I once facilitated an adult religious/spiritual education class called "Articulating Your Faith," named after a book by the same title.[51] We weren't long into sharing the basics and origins of our individual faith journeys when one man said, "I wish I had a story."

He went on to explain that he hadn't been brought up in a particular faith tradition, and was now feeling the absence of a foundation upon which he could form and articulate his beliefs.

"I envy the fact that Christians and Jews and others who have been brought up formally in a particular religion have a common story to tell about what they believe. I wish I had that kind of story."

Every living thing has a story, and collectively these stories constitute a bigger story that has many renditions. Most of us have forgotten our stories. The purpose of our lives is to remember as much of the larger story of our existence as we can, and most importantly our particular narrative in it. Because our indigenous souls speak fluent "story," they can guide us on this remembering journey.

The noun "story" comes from the Old French *estoire* and the Late Latin *storia* (shortened from *historia*), meaning "story, chronicle, history, account, tale." A second meaning of this noun is "floor of a building" and also "picture," possibly due to the story-telling appearance of the facades of homes during the Middle Ages.

"Story," "historia" (a learning or knowing by inquiry), "history" (wise man, judge), and "vision" (to see, especially something supernatural) share a common PIE root: *weid-* which means "to know," or literally "to see," to have supernatural sight. To practice "story" (i.e., make this noun a verb), we use our supernatural powers of knowing and seeing, and then we tell our accounts of them.

As young children, we may have said to our parents, "Tell me a story." What we sought was an adult's account of something that we didn't have ourselves. A young child's world is small when it comes to lifetime experiences. To compensate, our imaginations are the greatest during those early years, and there is a great reliance on the adults' stories of events in the larger world.

When a child asks to be told a story, the child is literally requesting, "Tell me what you see. Give me a glimpse of the greater world out there that I don't know. Feed me that history."

As we grow older and learn more, our worlds expand such that we are more aware of relationships between others and ourselves, and our environment and ourselves. The request to our adult mentors now shifts from "Tell me *a* story" to "Tell me *the* story." The shift goes from "Tell me something I have no idea about" to "Explain to me the connection between myself and the things that I'm experiencing all around me."

"Tell me *the* story" indicates that the person is seeking guidance in understanding the existential questions that arise during our adolescence, make demands on us as adults, and carry us through our elder years unto death: "Who am I? Where did I come from?

What am I doing here (my purpose)? Where do I go from here (What happens when I die)?"

Collectively, these four questions will guide us in determining what *our* stories are, and they will help us point to what the larger story is.

The indigenous soul in each of us knows that our individual stories are bits and pieces of the larger story. Martin Prechtel explains, "Like life itself, the secret oneness of the 'Big Story' is in the overwhelming details of its diversity, where every little person, beast, wind, and misery is a necessary part of a greater churning dream. Every story is a dewdrop in the ocean of the 'Big Story.'"[52]

The Big Story is the container of all versions and episodes of human existence; of what it means to be a human being, and how to grow into one; of all the company and influence along the way; and all the dismembering and remembering that occurs.

Where do we go to find that "Big Story," and our unique place in it?

Creation stories provide a fascinating start. These are our ancestors' accounts of how and where they originated on earth, and the stories were passed along from generation to generation through the oral tradition for which indigenous populations are so well known. In reading or listening to these ancient stories, many of their details may sound like fairy tales or science fiction. Who knows what actually happened, and what is embellished? What creation stories offer us are the common themes about human existence that can be traced through potentially hundreds of different versions of creation stories.

In her book *Primal Myths*, Barbara Sproul writes that creation myths are the most comprehensive and profound sources of the answers to human existential questions: "Who am I? How do I fit into the worlds of society and nature? How should I live?"[53]

Because these questions are just as pertinent today as they were thousands and thousands of years ago, these creation stories are timeless. And whether we realize it or not, these stories have shaped us. Our ancestors told them to their children and grandchildren and great-grandchildren, laying the foundation for who we are and how we live today.

If this is hard to imagine, think about the influence that the story of Adam and Eve has had on our entire planet. Even if you don't identify yourself as a Christian or a Jew, you live in a world where Christian missionizing over many centuries has spread the interpretation of the first couple's expulsion from the Garden of Eden as humanity's fall from God's grace. As a result, the insidious message that humans are flawed and broken has infused if not driven the development and implementation of public policies at micro- and macro-levels for centuries. It is reasonable to think that other creation stories have similarly influenced other cultures' rules and guidelines for optimal individual and societal functioning.

Another source for finding our places in the larger Story is our elders. Story telling was a very sacred practice for our ancestors, and it has maintained that holy status not only among First Nations peoples, but also within many organized religions. Perhaps in our current high-tech lives we've lost the magic of storytelling to TV shows and movies, relinquishing to screenwriters the complete responsibility of telling stories that inform us and remind us of who we are.

Our indigenous souls long for the continuation of human-to-human, face-to-face storytelling. We can satisfy that longing by asking of our elders, "Tell me *the* story of how your grandparents came to America;" "Tell me *the* story of the town that is named after my great-great-uncle;" or "Tell me AGAIN and AGAIN *the* story of the night I was born. I never tire of it!"

And then let us listen. To the stories shared by our families and friends, let us listen and honor and validate. From the stories they share, let us learn more about one another, and ponder together our common and uncommon origins and destinies. Let us listen intently to the spoken words, as their vibrations reach wider into the atmosphere than we realize, and feed many an ancestor that we never knew.

Two other sources of information about our personal stories are our DNA, and our Akashic Records. Tracking one's ancestry and roots via DNA testing has become popular and accessible in the recent past, revealing decades if not centuries of story. Results can be life-changing, as individuals realize how diverse their family background is. In many cases, personal prejudices have had to be re-examined when individuals realized that the very group they held a bias against was actually part of their own ancestry.

Akashic Records, also known as "The Book of Life," are the energetic histories or records of all souls that have ever existed. Although this information source is ancient, it didn't become well-known in the modern Western culture until the late 1800s, and was probably most popularized by Edgar Casey in the early 1900s. These Records can be thought of as a massive, holographic computer system, sometimes referred to as "the mind of God," that contains all the data from every single lifetime of every single soul.

The data in the Records includes not just the events that happened in a particular life, but also every thought, feeling, and intention that occurred in every lifetime. It is not for the purpose of judging or condemnation, but rather an endless bank of information that can help people learn about themselves and their relationships in the context of what the purposes of their earthly lives are. Accessing ones Akashic Records is possible through meditative states, either self-guided or facilitated by a medium.

Whether through Creation stories or modern storytelling, through DNA, or Akashic Records readings, learning one's story is a process of reconciliation ("to make friendly again, to reconnect"), whereby we remember connections that we forgot existed from earlier lives, making friendly to us once again all the patterns and purposes of our lives.

We've all got story in us. We were born with it, and into it. We were fed by it, we've learned it, and yet we're still remembering. Our daytime and nighttime dreams are stories about us and for us, and so we pay attention to them. It seems our stories pursue us even as we pursue them, so the reunion is inevitable. As we remember, that is, put together, our stories, let us carry the mantle of Storyteller, sharing what we see and know.

Reflect

1. Using the floors of a building analogy, what are the stories that make up *your* story?
2. What does "true story" mean to you? Can a story be true? Or does the word "story" mean it's not true?
3. On the Internet, look up the John Hiatt song, "Seven Little Indians." Listen to it while you read the lyrics. Then listen to it three more times with your eyes closed. During the first, be the Chief; then be the wife; and finally, be the little Indians. Did it make you feel the importance of story in a new way?

Practice

1. Spend time with the existential questions of *your* story: Who am I? Where did I come from? What am I doing here (my purpose)? Where do I go from here (when I die)?
    *   Keep a journal where you can write your thoughts about each of these questions.
    *   As these questions arise again and again in your life, don't ignore them. Go to your journal.
    *   Be prepared that your answers will be revised over time, as situations in your life elicit new perspectives from you.
    *   Be prepared also that your answers may end up generating more questions. Don't get overwhelmed; go with the flow.
    *   Remember that there's no endpoint where you conclude, "That's my story, and I'm stickin' to it!" Like you, your story is alive and unfolding.

2. Ask your elders to tell you stories, including *the* stories that bind you to them.

3. Tell your children and grandchildren stories, especially *the* stories that bind them to you.

4. What do you consider to be your culture's Creation Story? Explore other cultures' creation stories, and compare them with yours.

5. Research your ancestry.

6. Research the meaning and accessibility of the Akashic Records, and consider tapping into this infinite resource to learn more about your story.

7. Celebrate your successful practice.

8. Repeat as needed.

20

BEAUTIFY

Beauty is before me, and Beauty behind me.
Above me and below me hovers the beautiful.
I am surrounded by it.
I am immersed in it.
In my youth, I am aware of it.
And in old age, I shall walk quietly the beautiful trail.
In beauty it is begun.
In beauty, it is ended.

−Diné Prayer Chant

Our indigenous souls know, unquestionably and reverently, three things about beauty: (1) that we were born into a beautiful world, (2) that we were born beautiful and will die beautiful, and (3) that we were born with the capacity and desire for making beauty while we're here. Accordingly, this chapter focuses on knowing beauty, being beauty, and making beauty.

"Beauty" comes from the PIE root *deu-*, meaning, "to do, perform; show favor, revere." From this same root comes the prefix *bene-*, which means, "well, in the right way, honorably, properly." It appears by these origins that beautifying is at once something to admire and appreciate as well as something to do. In addition, beauty exudes a quality of natural perfection that is perceived and respected.

To know beauty is to recognize that it is all around us, and to be grateful for the gift of it. The Diné chant gives voice to our innate understanding that beauty is everywhere, enveloping us from every direction. If we are blind to this reality, then we don't stand a chance of knowing how beautiful we are ourselves, or of how capable we are of making beauty. This would place us out of balance with the natural beauty of Earth, and so the Diné chant is both an acknowledgement of Mother Earth's perfect beauty *and* a prayer that one may benefit from a lifetime walk that is in sync with that sacred planetary balance. It is recognition that beauty is the beginning and ending of our lives as well as the life of the planet. Beauty is the indigenous version of Alpha and Omega.

"In my youth, I am aware of it. And in old age, I shall walk quietly the beautiful trail." We all intuitively knew beauty as children, and frolicked in it unabashedly. And many of us rediscover its vitality in our elder years. But in between, beauty seems to go dormant. In our Western culture, we are typically uninhibited by the beauty we experience *and* create as children, and this is also true when we become elders. As children, we don't know any better than to be our natural selves; and as elders we remember and revive our natural selves because we come to realize that we've got nothing to lose now *but* our selves. During our adulthood, we may fall out of balance with beauty, as the premium on productivity and success takes over, squelching the artist in each of us.

It is in these years that the beauty-killing messages we received along the way take hold—that art is a luxury, not a necessity, and artists can't pay their bills; that there's a fantasy world and a real world, and only the latter offers security; that we can't sing or dance; that we're not as artistic as so-and-so, and who do we think we are, anyway, claiming to be a beauty maker? And we believed them.

Another prevailing notion that arrested our beauty development has been the centuries-old indoctrination that we humans are imperfect, flawed, and therefore not beautiful. Yet, how could we not be anything but gorgeously beautiful, if All is One, and we are made of God-stuff?

We are perfectly, beautifully us! If All is One, then each of us is a unique manifestation or reflection of the One, perfectly. Each of us is a beautiful creation, and perfectly beautiful. Mother Earth calls us her own, and asks us to walk in sync with her and "live our lives as works of art"[54] while we're walking. The saying, "It takes one to know one!" is appropriate here – it takes beauty to know beauty. In order for us to recognize and appreciate beauty all around us, we must recognize and appreciate our own beauty.

Another way to say it is the common adage, "Beauty is in the eyes of the beholder." If we know beauty when we see it, hear it, taste it, smell it, or sense it in any way, it's because we, the beholders, are beautiful!

As for making beauty, we humans are built just right for this task. Our anatomy provides all the tools we need to beautify. There's an African saying that goes, "If you can walk, you can dance. If you can talk, you can sing." Our feet and our voices are instruments of beauty. A Maya understanding is that the Holies, in creating humans, gave us the special gifts of thumbs and tongues—the gods themselves didn't even have them! Instead, they made thumbs and tongues part of our bodies so that we would make beauty. Think of how much beauty we are capable of making with our thumbs and our tongues! The beauty we are called to make with our hands and voices is food to humans and Holies alike. We are called to be the artists that we are.

The word "art" comes from the PIE root *ar-, meaning, "fit together, join." So an artist is one who joins or fits things together. In the literal sense this takes place when we create or build material things—we are combining materials together to form a beautiful product, such as a song, a painting, a display, a garment, a bouquet, or a home.

And, in the figurative sense, art refers to how making beauty reveals the interconnectedness between everything and everyone. Beauty joins us together. Making beauty binds and unites us, indeed saves us.

I remember a time in my young adulthood when I was deeply saddened by a calamity that caused great harm to many people. The news coverage lasted for weeks. Even though I wasn't directly affected, I was certainly participating in the collective grief. I didn't know what to do with that grief. I called my mother and told her about it, and sought her advice. She told me, "Do something with your hands. Bake some bread. Do some cross-stitch. Plant something. Play an instrument. Just do something with your hands."

I've never forgotten her advice, and I've followed it many times. I've always found making something with your hands to be grounding and soothing in situations like this, when you know you can't *fix* what has happened. I know now that it was all about making beauty.

And the first time I followed my mother's advice, I remember thinking, "Right now I'm in good company with everyone else around the world who is also making bread at this moment. Together, we are keeping the world going."

It would be negligent not to mention the flip side of beauty-making art. From the same PIE root comes "arm" ("upper limb, elbow; joint, shoulder"); and it turns out that etymologically speaking, "art" is related to the Latin term *arma,* which means "weapons." As we know, the term "arms" is often used to mean "weapons." What this means is that all of our innate and anatomical tools for making beauty are equally capable of inhibiting or even destroying beauty. The choice is ours: for what are we going to use our arms, our hands and feet, our tongues and thumbs?

We've got all we need in us and around us to know, be, and make beauty. So, as natural born artists, let's keep the world going with the beauty we make.

Reflect

1. "Beauty is in the eyes of the beholder." When you look in the mirror, do you see beauty?
2. What constitutes beauty in our Western culture? Which examples do you agree with, and which ones do you disagree with?
3. When was the last time you:
   - Created something with your own hands?
   - Sang out loud or danced, or both?
   - Stared at cloud formations?
   - Bought art, or something to make art, for yourself?
   - Cooked a meal from scratch?
   - Told someone that they were beautiful?
   - Believed someone when they told you that you are beautiful?

Practice

1. Know beauty:
   - As often as you can during your waking hours, look above, below, and around you to experience the beauty that surrounds you. Note its visual appearances, its smells and tastes, its textures, and its sounds.
   - Welcome the feelings that arise in you when you experience beauty.
   - Acknowledge and say "thank you" to the beauty's source.
2. Be beauty:
   - Smile a lot, especially in public places.
   - Dress and carry yourself as beautiful, because you are.
   - Remember that being beautiful is not a selfish or self-centered position, unless it is used to make someone else feel ugly. Be beautiful in ways that not only permit but also encourage others to be as beautiful as they are.

3. Make beauty:
    - Be the artist that you naturally are. If you think you're not, look up "How to Be an Artist" by SARK, and allow her to change your mind.
    - Treat yourself to lessons or training in art, music, dance, flower arranging, weaving, carpentry, or a similar beauty-making endeavor.
    - Decorate your home and workplace in ways that those spaces where you spend most of your life reflect beauty. Your family and colleagues will thank you, and so will the rooms you decorated!
    - Tell people how beautiful they are.
4. Celebrate your successful practice.
5. Repeat as needed.

21

BLESS

May the warm winds of heaven blow softly upon your house. May the Great Spirit bless all who enter there. May your moccasins make happy tracks in many snows, and may the rainbow always touch your shoulder.

–Cherokee Blessing

"God bless America!" can be heard at patriotic events. "God bless this food," often precedes a meal. "Blessed be," may conclude a prayer." And, we hear Christmas revelers quote Tiny Tim, "God bless us, everyone!" But what does it mean to bless, who can do it, and why is it so important to our indigenous souls?

The word "bless" comes from the Old English word *bletsian*, "To consecrate, make holy, give thanks." *Bletsian* comes from the Proto-Germanic **blodison*, which means, "hallow with blood, mark with blood." Our understanding of "bless" as "to praise, speak well of" originates out of these two words. In addition, a different meaning can be found in the deeper origins of "bless."

The PIE root of the Old English and Proto-Germanic words is **bhlo-to-*, which is thought to mean, "to swell, gush, spurt," thus the association with blood. But a precursor of that root is **bhel-*, which means, "to thrive, bloom;" "to blow, inflate or swell," or "blossom, flourish."

Together, these original meanings indicate that to bless is simultaneously a spiritual and a physical act, bridging the sacred and the profane. To be blessed is to thrive and flourish in the understanding of the divinely given life force that sustains you. To bless something or someone is to bestow (gush, spurt) that same understanding upon others.

Our lives are gifts. We didn't earn them or request them; they were given to us. To be born is to receive one's first and perpetual divine favor. This was our first blessing, what Matthew Fox calls "Original Blessing."[55] From that moment on, we have been blessed with a place to live, be fed, grow, relate, belong, learn, and remember, and that place is Mother Earth.

As recipients of countless blessings, we also are automatically deputized to bless: To whom much is given, from them much is required. Just as with all of the other practices in this book, blessing keeps the world going. Because each of us embodies the holy within us, we have the authority and capacity to bless. And because we are all One—all in this together—we have the responsibility to bless.

From an indigenous perspective, blessing is a way of dissolving 3rd Dimension barriers. For starters, it exposes separation for what it is, an illusion. The essence of blessing is relationship, and its product is reunion. To bless and be blessed is to connect, and to recognize and sanctify that we belong *in* this world and *to* each other. When you bless someone, you *belong* them to you, claiming them as blood brother/sister. A blessing is like a spiritual blood donation!

Blessing is the antithesis of judging, blaming, rejecting, resisting, and all other forms of disempowering and disenfranchising. Instead, mutual authenticity and vulnerability are the necessary conditions for a blessing to be given or received.

Blessings are by nature all-inclusive. Because everything is alive energetically, ALL are eligible to give and receive blessings. That means that we can bless and be blessed by people we don't even know. This happens all the time when we pray for someone that we've never met. In this regard, blessings are like door prizes that you don't have to be present to win!

What this means, however, is that we are responsible for blessing people we don't particularly like or who are on a path that feels unacceptable or uncomfortable to us. There is a familiar saying, "There, but for the grace of God, go I." Essentially that statement proclaims, "That could be *me* suffering that situation; I thank God it's not!" But the Law of One would have that familiar saying altered dramatically, to say simply: "There go I."

If we find it difficult to find the love inside ourselves to bless those who disturb us to some degree, we need to remember that we and the people who disturb us are One. The person we don't feel like blessing is us. What we learned about love and forgiveness is also true of blessing: If we can't bring ourselves to bless another being, it means we're unwilling to bless ourselves. And if we don't feel deserving of our own blessings, we will fail to see others as deserving as well.

So-called inanimate objects are also worthy of and eligible for blessings. We do it all the time and may not even realize it. The obvious examples are the elements we use in rituals, such as earth, water, air, and fire; bread and wine; wedding rings; anointing oils; and sacred writings. Think of the items in your possession that you consider sacred, from which you draw strength during difficult times: symbols, plaques, jewelry or clothing, photos, artwork. Once blessed, these items hold sacred power that then continue to bless whenever they are revisited.

In his book, *To Bless the Space Between Us*, John O'Donahue attests to the power of these objects in our lives: "There is certain poignancy in this belief that blessing can enter the silence and privacy of the object and continue to dwell there. It changes the nature of the object; it is no longer simply itself. Now it is a live sanctuary from which the divine light and protection proceed."[56]

Because they never expire, blessings also dissolve the 3rd Dimension aspect of time. "Give thanks for unknown blessings already on their way" is a Native American saying that exemplifies this truth. In that brief directive, the future is pulled into the present, such that the receiver is already experiencing the blessings that haven't yet arrived. And how does the author of that statement know that there are blessings on their way? Most likely, it's because blessings have made their way to him before. Past, present, and future are happening all at once: he presently remembers past blessings that found him, and presently knows that more are coming. He advises us to do the same.

Imagine how wonderful that feels to be forever blessed! When we know this to be undoubtedly true, only then will we be able to bless our way through every moment and day of our lives. When we embody our blessedness, we will find it easy to bless even the alarm clock that awakens us to the gift of another day, the dirty dishes in the sink that indicate that we're not going hungry, Monday mornings that make us grateful for the meaningful work of our bodies and minds, the bills in our mailboxes that remind us of our dependency on others to sustain our ways of living, the late-night phone call that tests and strengthens the bonds of family and friends, and even the sufferings we endure that have us confessing to and calling upon the unseen holy forces at work on our behalf. When we feel eternally blessed, there isn't anyone or anything in our lives from which we should hold back our blessings.

As we perform our blessing duties, it's important to remember that we have received blessings without earning them, and we should have no expectations about return on the blessings we offer. As dispensers of blessings, we must fully realize that we are carriers and channels of divine love, not creators of it. We can no more take credit for the origin of that love than we can for our very existence. So, blessing is not a quid-pro-quo transaction; rather, it is indebtedness being paid forward.

If our blessings are not well-received by someone, let that not rob us of our own peace and good will, and let it not cause the illusion of separation to reappear. Let us not take the rejection personally. Let us neither carry any malice toward them nor let their malice prevent us from blessing. Instead, let us bless them *anyway*, even if they appear unreasonable, jealous, dishonest, thoughtless, mean, or just oblivious. Let us bless them *especially*, because their need for reunion with divine love is great.

As the place where soul meets soul in the intertwining of sacred and profane, blessings make holy ground out of wherever we are standing. When we bless, we are calling in, invoking, the spirit realm to shine its favor on something or someone. Invocation is the language of blessing, and mercy is its dialect. Out of pure kindness and utter devotion, we call in the divine to make holy this very moment, this being in front of us, this action taking place.

With rare exception, the word "may" is always found in the first few words of any blessing. As both a request and a statement, we are at once inviting the divine AND carrying out the request, making it so. To bless is to be ambassadors of the Holies and advocates for all of life that we claim as kin.

There's not much that blessings can't accomplish. They help us to perceive togetherness out of alienation; goodness out of depravity; vision out of blindness; hope out of despair; and recovery out of loss. They heal, welcome, embrace, rejuvenate, validate, gather and build, energize and synergize. And as John O'Donahue tells us, they inspire us to "have the courage today to live the lives that we would love, to postpone our dreams no longer, to waste our hearts on fear no more, and to do at last what we came here for."[57] Blessing, among other things, is what we came here for.

Reflect

1. Reflect on your own experiences of blessing or of being blessed.

- Has this been common practice in your life?
- What was the most memorable blessing you received? What made it so memorable?
- Did you feel changed by the blessing you received? What did it do for you?
- How comfortable are you in giving blessings?

2. Reflect on the sacred objects you have in your home. What makes them sacred, and what do they offer you?

Practice

1. See every day acts and routines as opportunities for blessings. This is also known as making the ordinary sacred. Obvious examples include mealtimes, and special occasions like rites of passage. But consider that a blessing would be entirely appropriate for someone's first day of school or a new job; for your pet before its trip to the vet; for an instrument before it is played; for a birthday card before it is dropped into the mailbox; and so many more.

2. Here's some guidance on crafting your own blessings:
- "May" is a key word in the beginning of blessings.
  - Think of the blessing you want to give as a wish or hope for the person or thing you're blessing. For example, "I hope you learn some fun things at school today" could be stated this way as a blessing: "May your day at school be fun, and the things that you learn amaze you."
  - The blessing can be brief and simple, such as the example above; or it can be lengthier in addressing multiple aspects of the particular occasion.
  - Concluding the blessing with "So be it" or "And so it is" acknowledges the authority of the one who gives the blessing, and at the same time points to that person's faith in the spiritual realm to make the blessing come true. It's an affirmation and an invocation at the same time.

3. Remember that you don't have to be a minister or imam or shaman to offer a blessing. You simply have to be human.

4. Research and collect resources that provide blessings. Quote them, or modify them with adaptations that fit your own unique situations.

5. Don't hesitate to ask for blessings. Receiving blessings is every bit as unifying and reconciling as giving them.

6. Celebrate your successful practice.

7. Repeat as needed.

22

SIMPLIFY

Look and listen for the welfare of the whole people and have always in view not only the present but also the coming generations, even those whose faces are yet beneath the surface of the ground—the unborn of the future nation.

–The Constitution of the Iroquois Nation
(The Great Binding Law)

"Keep it simple, stupid!" and "It's complicated!" are modern-day mantras in our fast-paced, high-tech lives. Many of us long for a simpler and more manageable existence, yet we may not feel sufficiently empowered to accomplish a slow-down in our routines and a reduction in the number of our commitments and obligations. If we feel overwhelmed with how complicated society has become, it's our indigenous souls trying to get our attention.

"Simplify" comes from two Latin words: *simplex* ("simple") and *facere* ("to make"). *Simplex* is made up of two PIE roots: **sem-* ("one, as one, together with") and **plek-* ("to plait, braid, twist, fold"). The PIE root of *facere* is *dhe-* ("to put, to set, to do"). Literally speaking, to simplify is to put things together as one, in a braided, folded way. Generally speaking, to simplify is to weave together similar things into a fabric of one.

"Complicated" comes from the Latin word *complicates*, and means "folded together, confused, intricate." It's easy to see the similar word structure and word origins between "simplify" and "complicate"—both have the same PIE root *plek-*. So the etymological difference between the words, although subtle, is in their prefixes. *Sim-* means "same," where *com-* means "together." Etymologically speaking, there doesn't seem to be a big difference. But practically speaking, there is. To simplify is to weave together threads that are like each other, the same. To complicate is to weave together threads that are not necessarily like each other.

A term often used interchangeably with "simple" is "easy," yet these two words really do not have the same meaning. "Easy" comes from the Old French word *aisie*, which means "comfortable, at ease, rich, well-off." "Ease" means "free from bodily discomfort and anxiety." Simplifying makes no mention of how difficult or uncomfortable it is to do so; rather, it directs how to do something and informs the shape it will take. So it's not only possible, but also likely, that simplifying is not an easy thing to do. However, a simplified life, once established, will more than likely be easier to maintain than a complicated one.

Practically speaking, these word origins and meanings direct us to examine our lifestyles and daily routines to assess coherence (literally "stuck together") or congruency (literally "agreement, fitted together").

Are the commitments that we maintain, the demands that we agree to meet, and the values we hold congruent with each other? Are they the "same," as we weave them together? And further, are they congruent with Cosmic Law? If so, then the braid that is our daily life will hold together more easily. Each strand will support the other in likeness and the strands will be in sync with Cosmic Law. The weave of our lives will look and feel streamlined, efficient, and holistic.

In contrast, what would the result be if our commitments,

demands, and values are not the same—or are the same, but not coherent with Universal Law—yet have been woven together anyway? The weave isn't as coherent or robust, and it will require more attention and energy to keep the fabric of our lives from tearing or unraveling. Complicated lives are high maintenance, so it's worth considering the compromises and costs that will have to be made to sustain them, and how our indigenous souls will fare.

Malidoma Somé identifies two ubiquitous and defining forces in the modern Westernized world that threaten or challenge a simplified lifestyle: technology and speed.[58] "Technology" ("systematic treatment of an art, craft, or technique") is made up of *techno-* and *-logy*; the former comes from the PIE root **teks-* ("to weave, fabricate, make"), and the latter means "a speaking, discourse, treatise, doctrine, theory, science." A related term, "machine," comes from the PIE word **maghana-* ("that which enables"), from the PIE root **magh-* ("to be able, have power"). Collectively these terms refer to technology as discussing and learning ways that give us the power to make things.

"Speed" comes from the Old English word *sped*, which means "success, prosperity, riches, wealth; luck; opportunity, advancement." It comes from the PIE root **spe-*, "to thrive, prosper." Where technology refers simply to the ability to make something, speed refers to one's economic status because of its association with success and material wealth.

The difference in these two terms may well represent the distinction between the indigenous mindset and the Westernized mindset regarding the value it places on technology. The indigenous soul welcomes and embraces technology that can help people remember and fulfill their life purpose and benefit the whole village, or even the whole planet. In contrast, the Westernized competition-driven culture places a premium on technology that speeds up processes and, intentional or not, advances some individuals ahead of others.

The forces of technology and speed are not inherently good or bad. They are neutral. But they are energetic forces, and are therefore alive. Our indigenous souls know this, but our 3rd Dimensional consciousness is oblivious to this fact, perceiving machines to be inanimate objects made of inanimate materials. But machines, being alive, will only respond according to how and what we feed them.

This is true even of non-automated tools as well. Once when I was in a village setting, I was helping others harvest corn in a ceremonial way, honoring the life of the corn and the life/death cycle that was necessary for the germination and growing of the corn. Even with my reverent intent, a fellow participant abruptly halted my efforts when I opened by pocketknife and started to cut the stalk.

"Wait!" she warned, "you forgot to do something before you start cutting."

She then explained that before I put the blade to anything, I first had to ask for its willingness to participate in this ceremony of corn harvesting. Equally important, I had to also inform the knife that my intentions for its use were all life-honoring, not life-dishonoring. The purpose of doing this was to *feed* the knife with my positive intentions and thoughts so that we would be on the "same" energetic wavelength with each other and with Mother Nature as we partnered in the corn-harvesting ceremony.

The old computer programming warning rings true here: "Garbage in, garbage out." Similarly, "It's the thought that counts."

So when it comes to using technology and modes of speed, it all comes down to this: What is the intent? If our purposes of the uses of these modalities are in sync with Natural Laws, then it can be accurately said that they have simplified our lives and rendered them sustainable. But if our purposes run counter to Natural Law, then we've just made our lives and Mother Nature's life complicated, and ultimately unsustainable. Technology and speed that run counter to Natural Law will backfire on our machines, our environment, and us. There is ample proof of this in our world today.

Reflect

1. What does the chapter's opening quote have to do with simplifying one's life? In other words, what influence does simplifying your life have on future generations?
2. Do you have a situation in your life right now that you would call "complicated?" How would you "simplify" it?
3. How does technology enrich your life? How does it impoverish it?
4. Can you think of an example of a change that you made in your life that was *simple,* but not *easy*?

Practice

1. Ask these questions about your use of speedy and technological devices, non-automated tools, and even your actions and thoughts:
   • Is this life-honoring vs. life dishonoring?
   • Is this in sync with Cosmic Law and Mother Nature?
   • Is this congruent with my values?
2. If the answer to any of these questions is "no," here is some guidance on how to rectify the situation:
   • Review the Practice sections in Chapters 13 (Shed), 15 (Yield), and 17 (Respond).
   • Organize ("construct, establish") your life, incorporating the necessary changes. "Organize" comes from the word "organ," which literally means "that with which one works." The PIE root of "organ" is *werg-* ("to do"). Essentially this means, organize your life according to how it works for you and Mother Nature simultaneously.
   • Stay in present time when discerning how to organize your life. Dwelling in the future is typically fear-based, and dwelling in the past is often regret- or guilt-based.

- Look inside you for what you seek outside of you: wisdom, joy, satisfaction, bliss, courage, and more.

3. Try your hand at simplifying the following examples, letting the knife in the corn harvesting ceremony example be a guide:
    - An automobile
    - A computer, tablet, or cell phone
    - A gun in the home (HINT: You may have to do a little research on ancestral/indigenous ways of hunting, and how they differ from modern ways.)

4. Celebrate your successful practices.

5. Repeat as needed.

23

BALANCE

Great Mystery, teach me how to trust my heart, my mind, my intuition, my inner knowing, the senses of my body, the blessings of my spirit. Teach me to trust these things so that I may enter my Sacred Space and love beyond my fear, and thus walk in balance with the passing of each glorious sun.

–Lakota Prayer

There's never been a time during humankind's existence when balance wasn't an important component of being fully human, but in this age of ascension, it is more critical than ever before. Earth's vibratory levels continue to increase, and we humans need to increase our vibratory level as well, in order to accompany Her without suffering symptoms of imbalance. Balancing not only helps us vibrate at a higher level, but it also helps us clear out all the lower vibration residues that served us well in the 3rd Dimension, but will now only impede our ascension because they are not compatible with the higher Dimensions.

Where "simplify" focused on similarity (i.e., "same"), "balance" is concerned with equality. As a verb, "balance" means, "be equal with; bring or keep in equilibrium." As a noun, it means "apparatus for weighing," possibly from two Latin words: *bis* ("twice") and *lanx* ("dish, plate, scale of a balance"). "Equilibrium" is made up of *equi-* ("equal") and *–librium* (from *libra*, Latin for "a balance; a pair of scales"). The aim in balancing, then, is to make sure that one part doesn't outweigh any other part, causing the whole to become unstable. Acknowledging that each part of the whole is of equal importance, the aim of balancing is to give equal attention to each part of oneself.

However, this works better on paper than it does in real life, because the parts are all so intertwined with each other. It would be impossible to isolate one aspect or part of oneself to give attention to exclusively, because other interrelated parts would also be affected. For example, if I decide that I want to improve my physical health by exercising, I find that it doesn't just benefit my anatomy and physiology. While I'm exercising, I'm reducing my stress level, and my emotional health improves. Additionally, while exercising I think about the movie I attended last night with my friends, and my mental health improves as I remember our various interpretations of the movie's meanings. My spiritual health is also enhanced, as I contemplate how grateful I am for my friends, for my physical ability to exercise, and for the countless blessings in my life.

Therefore, to find and maintain balance in our lives, we must take into account how integrated all the parts, Dimensions, densities, and energies are within the human body. "Integrate" ("to render something whole, bring together its parts") comes from the Latin word *integer*, which literally means "untouched." The PIE roots of *integer* are *in-* ("not") and **tag-* ("to touch, handle). Figuratively, something integrated is "untainted, upright," whole and robust in a pristine, natural way, that needn't be improved by tampering or meddling with it. That's the type of balance we are capable of, and called on to maintain, one that emulates the natural balance of things in nature. Our indigenous souls remember how imbalance manifests itself in the physical forms of disease. Healing, then, focuses on recovering balance within oneself, and between oneself and the overall life force.

Generally speaking, the balancing that is required of us relates to our ability to shift our mode of perceiving and being in the world from 3rd Dimension consciousness into 4th and 5th Dimension consciousness. A deeper exploration into the characteristics of these Dimensions is provided in the Coordinate chapter and Appendix B, but for now we focus on one example from the Table in Appendix B - "Dichotomy." To balance ourselves for ascension, we must be willing to move from seeing things as opposites to seeing them as integrated. Think of the Yin-Yang image that not only has the two sides balanced with each other, but additionally each half contains within itself a piece of the so-called opposite side. So for example, feminine and masculine energies do not oppose each other, but rather seek to be in balance with each other *and* integrated with one another. The same is true of the secular or seen world compared to the spiritual or unseen world—they do not compete with each other. Rather, they depend on and affect each other, and often merge. If one of them is given too much attention over the other one, imbalance will occur.

The Yin-Yang symbol not only indicates how each one is a part of the other, it also illustrates how one side of the polarity can't be recognized without the other side's contrast. The dark and light sections of the symbol are clearly visible because of the contrast with the other. Such contrasts exist all around us in life. Here's a practical example: Try using a flashlight in broad daylight, and you'll find it is useless. This is because darkness is required as a contrast for the light from the flashlight to be visible.

The balance point between the two aspects of a dichotomy (e.g. light and dark) is called neutrality. Think of a see-saw or a weighing scale in which the two sides are in balance—each at the same height. This is the place of balance that is desired in all aspects of our lives. This is particularly important to remember when we attempt to defeat or eliminate altogether an aspect that is deemed "bad." For example, while it may seem to be virtuous to eliminate evil, it is not only unrealistic, but it's not practical. If all evil were eliminated, we wouldn't know what good is. If we eliminated all sadness, joy would become mundane, and thus *not* joy. If we eliminated death, the meanings of our lives would dwindle and vanish. If you cut off one end of the see-saw, the other side loses its function, and there wouldn't be a see-saw anymore!

As we bring in this new age, we must find that neutral place as we embrace the stimuli of our lives, especially the trying ones. It will require each of us to consider both sides of a situation and integrate its wholeness into ours. By doing so, we can accomplish coherence between our lives and the web of our planetary existence.

Reflect

1. Reflect on your own life regarding balance: what parts of your life do you feel are in balance, and what parts are not?
2. Think of a time when you took action to remedy an imbalance in your life.
   - What was imbalanced?
   - What action did you take?
   - Was balance restored?
3. Now think of a time when you ignored an imbalance in your life until it caused significant detriment to you.
   - What did you learn?
   - How did you respond?
4. Compare and contrast how you feel when you're resting in the neutrality zone of a situation vs. clinging to one side or pole of the situation.
   - Which location is calmer, and which has more drama?
   - Which location offers a better setting for learning more about yourself and the world you live in?

Practice

In Appendix A, the Maya Coordinates show the Dimensions-based physical, emotional, mental, and spiritual planes of a human being. Although practices aimed at one plane also enhance the others, here are some practices recommended for each plane:

1. Physical plane:
   * A balanced diet includes fresh local food; is primarily or completely vegetarian; has little or no sugar and salt; and has water as the primary source of fluid intake.
   * Alcohol or other drugs are to be limited or avoided.
   * Natural remedies are recommended over synthetic ones; and lifestyle changes are generally recommended over medicines administered into the body.
   * Cleansing and purifying, e.g. fasting, sweat lodges, ceremonial dancing and chanting, are good ways to re-establish balance.
   * Daily movement is necessary, such as cardio–respiratory activity, or breathing and balance exercises, such as qigong or yoga.
   * Enjoy rest, sleep, and relaxation on a non-artificial schedule, e.g., no alarm clock; going to bed when tired and waking when rested.

2. Emotional plane:
   * Follow the practices in Chapters 11 (Feel) and 16 (Love) that increase your vibration, moving your emotional energy up into your higher chakras.
   * Balance social connections with some solitary time. Chapters 4 and 5 (Inter-depend, and Belong) can help you with the former; and Chapters 7, 8, and 24 (Remember, Intuit/Dream, and Pray) may help you with the latter.

3. Mental plane:
    *   A variety of energetic modalities serve to balance mental energies, including but not limited to: PSYCH K, Reiki, EFT (emotional freedom technique, a.k.a tapping), TFT (thought field therapy), EMDR (eye movement and desensitization reprocessing), and Reconnective Healing.
    *   Study the "Dimensions" Table in Appendix B, and look for ways that you can challenge your perceptions and widen your perspectives on how the universe works.
    *   Review the practices in Chapters 6 (Learn), 7 (Remember), and 15 (Yield) to help you maintain mental balance.

4. Spiritual:
    *   Engage in a daily spiritual practice that does not adhere to the doctrinal and dogmatic aspects of religions, but instead to the mystical aspects of them.
    *   Review the practices in Chapters 8 (Intuit/Dream), 24 (Pray), and 29 (Rite) that take you into the spiritual realm.
    *   Trust your inner wisdom, and stay true to yourself at all times. Live a life of integrity and transparency, and act as if you wouldn't mind if people knew what you were thinking.
    *   Study the "Dimensions" Table in Appendix B, and look for ways that you can practice shifting your consciousness into higher Dimensions.

5. In Appendix C, the seven major chakras are illustrated and briefly explained. There are many ways to balance your chakras, and detailed information is widespread and accessible, so the recommendations provided here are general and brief. In addition, a Table in the Coordinate chapter, showing the life lessons and the Universal or Divine Law associated with each chakra, may help you understand how your life experiences affect your chakras. To balance the chakras, the

best practice is to embrace each experience as if it were a teacher who provides a lesson about your true self. If you are willing and able to do that, then collectively your chakras will become and remain balanced. There are a variety of approaches to balance individual chakras, but remember the aspect of integration—the body will be at its optimal balance when all seven chakras are open and active. Therefore, be careful not to neglect any of the chakras if you are taking the singular approach.

6. Celebrate your successful practices.
7. Repeat as needed.

24

PRAY

Every prayer is a seed planted in the Mystery. Each one addresses some aspect of our needs and urgings, and prepares the world in a mysterious way, as if it were a garden, for its fulfillment.

—Gabriel Horn

The thought of starting a daily prayer practice can be intimidating. A common excuse for not praying regularly is, "I don't know how to pray." Behind this one confession may hide these doubts: "I don't really know what prayer is;" "I don't know to whom or to what I am praying;" and "I don't know how I relate to the source I'm praying to." Prayer is such a mysterious and miraculous thing that some people are afraid of it, or they don't feel worthy or capable enough to enter into that realm. The etymology and ancient understandings of prayer can help us eliminate both of those barriers to an active prayer life.

"Pray" comes from the Latin word *precari* ("ask earnestly, beg, entreat") and the PIE root **prek-*, which means, "to ask, request, entreat." "Entreat" is made up of *en* ("in, into") and *–treat*, which comes from the PIE root **tragh-* ("to draw, drag, move"). Literally, to pray means to pull or draw into. Figuratively, praying is a process

138

of pulling into oneself the mysteries of existence, and being open to receive them.

For some, the object of prayer is "God;" for others it is "Creator," "Great Spirit," "Spirit of Life," "Collective Consciousness," or "Source." For some, it feels comfortable to enter into prayer saying, "Dear God, ..." For others it may feel more comfortable to enter into a quiet, still time and allow the spirit realm to become intimately known and felt. Thus, "meditation" and "contemplation" are terms often used to connote the same purpose, practice, and desired effect as prayer. So it's worth looking at the etymology of these two words as well.

"Meditate" comes from the Old French word *meditacion* ("thought, reflection, study"), and the PIE root *med- ("to measure, limit, consider, advise, take appropriate measures"). "Contemplation" comes from the Latin *contemplatio*, and originally meant, "to mark out a space for observation." "Temple" is closely related, and comes from the PIE root *tem-, meaning "to cut." To meditate or contemplate, literally, is to measure and cut out a specific place and time for observing and reflecting. When coupled with the meanings of "prayer" and "entreat," it can be summarized that praying is designating a time and place for the sole purpose of drawing the spirit world into us so that we may reflect and consider our cosmic connections.

Why is a regular prayer life important? As far as personal benefits, prayer is a necessary tool for maintaining balance, as it is the most significant way of attending to our spiritual plane. Prayer is also the doorway into the higher Dimensions of existence. When we pray, our vibratory rate increases, making it easier for us to elevate into 4th and 5th Dimension awareness. There is where we connect with the Holies, who yearn for our requests for their company and assistance in our 3rd Dimension, physical world. They long to help us remember how to be the spiritual beings that we are. The Holies entreat us as much as we entreat them, and they are as near as our very breath and heartbeat. But because of the Cosmic Law of Free Will, they cannot participate in our lives until we ask them. And that's what prayer does—it invokes them into action with us.

Prayer is not only a drawing of the spirit world into us it is also an acknowledgement of our own power that comes from the connection we have with Source or Creator. Each of us has within us a sliver of Source/Creator, connecting us and giving us the power to be co-creators. It is this very co-creative power within us that makes things manifest out of prayer.

As the opening quote points out, the Mystery is a garden waiting for our plantings of prayer. Therefore, like so many of the practices that are promoted in this book, prayer keeps the world going.

An active prayer life requires a number of things to sustain it. Of great importance, is a commitment to a specific time and place that is consistent from day to day, that is free of distraction. This should be considered so sacred a time that it is relatively non-negotiable. While the spirit world is available to us anytime we ask, the maintenance of a regular schedule will make the two-way communication between the two parties richer and more efficient.

What works for communication between two people works for communication between a human and the Holies: The more often there is conversation, the easier it is to resume where the communication ended the last time. The more attentive we are to the task at hand, the more effective the communication will be.

To begin the prayer or meditation time, it is recommended to "set the grid," which means to establish the energetic grounding for the communication that is about to occur. Here is an example, an adaptation of an opening prayer by Akemi G:

> I enter this space in love, light, and truth, and set the power grid accordingly. May all spirit guides who enter here also come in love, light, and truth; and may those who do not come in love, light, and truth be prohibited from entering.[59]

Such words set the stage for all benevolent beings to be available to us, without fear of any harmful encroachments.

Then, we need to address specifically whom we are praying to. This is a personal choice, and whom we invoke may vary depending on the situation.

We also need to clearly speak or write our intention. Is it simply to connect and be open to what the spirit realm brings us, i.e., passive meditation? Or is it a specific request for partnering with us in co-creating, i.e., active meditation? Both are legitimate and sacred purposes, but they are distinctly different. Passive meditation involves a clearing of the mind so that one can listen to what the Spirit realm communicates. Active meditation involves visualization for the purpose of effecting change.

There will be variations in what we perceive as a response. Sometimes it's related to what is going on internally, and sometimes it's related to the outer world. Remember that we are always connected with the Spirit realm, whether we feel it or not during prayer or meditation. Sometimes we may indisputably feel the connection, other times it may be undetectable. This is another reason why a daily practice is important.

The same etiquette we use for ending a phone conversation with a loved one is necessary as we end a prayer. We need to thank the spirit realm for interacting with us and for accompanying and aiding us as we strive to live spiritually in a physical world. And finally we need to "hang up," to bless the Holies on their way to accompany others who are also praying for their presence. An additional "See you tomorrow!" at the end will keep the spirit realm and us coming back for more.

Our indigenous souls know that prayer is a communal activity, because of its energetic nature. Even if we are alone when we are praying, our prayers join many others in the ether. As interdependent members of the human race, we are called on to pray *for* others, and *with* others. When we pray for others, we receive the benefit as well, for we are all One, spiritually.

Let us also remember that others are praying for us, and that we are beneficiaries of prayers from people we don't even know! Our prayers are further enhanced when we pray or meditate with others in a group setting. Praying in solitude does increase the vibratory level, but there is truth to the saying, "Wherever two or more are gathered . . . ." The benefit increases exponentially.

Because of the manifesting, co-creating power of prayer, we are also called on to observe particular times and places for prayer. There are certain times and dates that are considered sacred by people of many faith traditions, which especially call for prayer, e.g., religious holy days, and celestial events like lunar and solar episodes. Similarly, Elders and wisdom-keepers through the ages have identified sacred sites around the globe where the energy vortex is high, thereby further accentuating the power of prayer. Modern day shamans encourage us to find such places, and go to them and pray for peace.

Prayer on any scale is life-affirming and life-changing, making it one of the most important ways we can honor our indigenous souls. Ohi'ye S'a, a famous Native American of the Santee Dakota Tribe, said this about the necessity for prayer:

> In the life of the Indian there was only one inevitable duty—the duty of prayer—the daily recognition of the Unseen and the Eternal. His daily devotions were more necessary to him than daily food. He wakes at daybreak, puts on his moccasins, and steps down to the water's edge. He stands erect before the advancing dawn, facing the sun as it dances upon the horizon, and offers his unspoken orison. Each soul must meet the morning sun, the new sweet earth, and the Great Silence alone."[60]

May we honor his words and our indigenous souls with a prayer life that renders the Holies clamoring to join us.

Reflect

1. Is prayer or meditation a regular part of your day?
2. If you pray, to whom/what do you pray?
3. If you meditate, is it passive meditation, or active, or some of both?
4. What is (or would be) your ideal time and place for prayer or meditation?
5. How has prayer or meditation benefited your life?

Practice

1. Using some of the guidelines offered in this chapter, create your own prayer setting and style. Establish a regular practice that caters to both your schedule and your soul.
2. For starters, keep it simple: Say "please" to introduce what you seek; and "thank you" for all you have received.
3. Start your own collection of prayer books. There will be times that others' words of prayer will inspire you more than your own.
4. Research the locations and significance of ancient sacred sites, and consider visiting them to participate in solitary or group prayer.
5. Celebrate your successful practices.
6. Repeat as needed.

25

THANK

My barn having burned down, I can now see the moon.

−Mizuta Masahide

I remember many years ago seeing a bumper sticker that said, "If you can read this, thank a teacher." The spirit of this directive has infinite expressions, but they all emanate from this one: *If you were born, say, "thank you."* If you've been given life, an incarnation onto Earth, then you've been graced. Everything granted to us after that is icing on the cake. Each of us is born indebted, so may our every breath and every step be gratitude-soaked. Let "thank you" be our constant mantra.

"Thank" comes from the PIE root *tong-* ("to think, feel"), indicating that thanking is primarily an embodiment, and subsequently a verbal expression. To think and feel thanks is to be grateful. "Grateful" and "grace" both come from the PIE root *gwere-*, which means, "to favor." Our indigenous souls are keenly aware of the favor that was shown upon us by the Holies and the ancestors, who worked together diligently to bring us here. To be born in grace is to be intended, not random or accidental. It means there is a purpose for each of us; a place where we belong; and a people with whom we share our indebtedness. This is our original blessing, and so let all God's children say, "Thank you."

Lest we start feeling guilty for the lives and blessings we've been given without asking or earning them, gratitude is the better way. Gratitude is the antidote to sulking in a self-inflicted state of unworthiness. It is how we are called to respond, in ways that benefit all. Gratitude as a lifestyle is a way of paying forward the love that made our lives possible. Sooner *and* later, both givers *and* receivers of thanks are transformed. The more that gratitude is paid forward, the sooner it comes back to the original payer. Ultimately, gratitude enlightens us to the Universal Law of Oneness, as Hereditary Chief, Phil Lane Jr. explains:

> When we strive to make our lives, every thought, word and action, a living Wopida [Dakota word for gratitude], we are given a great spiritual gift. For whenever our soul and the inmost chambers of our heart are filled with thanksgiving and gratitude it also naturally becomes filled with compassion, love, understanding, forgiveness, joy, happiness and oneness. When our lives are centered in this State of Consciousness, there is no room left for the experience of fear, hate, prejudice, revenge, jealousy, loneliness and disunity. There is no room for anything that separates ourselves and our oneness with our Beloved Creator, our Human Family and all Life, seen and unseen.[61]

Thinking, feeling, and embodying gratitude allows us to see the world as a non-threatening place, if not a friendly one. Thus, it allows us to embrace the difficult times as well as the joyful ones. To live in a constant state of gratitude is to be able to enjoy the moon as it bears witness to the smoldering remains of the burned-down barn.

Meister Eckhart, the 13th Century theologian and mystic, said, "If the only prayer you ever say in your entire life is thank you, it will be enough." It's that simple, that short and sweet, and yet so powerful. Let not the brevity of Eckhart's advice and also of this chapter give the false impression that thanking is an insignificant or minor practice.

There are infinite ways in which we can demonstrate our gratitude for being alive. A number of the previous chapters are good examples, as are the next three.

Reflect

1. Do you consider yourself a grateful person? Why or why not?
2. Where does your sense of gratitude come from?
3. What does "grace" mean to you?

Practice

1. Say "thank you" to people for even the smallest things. People love to be thanked, don't you?
2. Via card, letter, phone, or social media – reach out to people you are grateful to have in your life. Tell them "thank you, for . . ." and be specific.
3. Every morning when you awaken, remember that not everyone made it through the night alive. Say "thank you" as your feet touch the floor.
4. When things aren't going well for you, say "thank you" for better times that came before, and the ones that are on their way.
5. Celebrate your successful practices.
6. Repeat as needed.

26

GIFT

An Indian's wealth is not measured by what he possesses, but rather what he gives away. For life to be rich and full, we must give as well as take.

–Robert Blackwolf Jones

"What can I bring?"

I'm sure that question didn't originate in southeast United States, but that's where I learned it. It was part of our southern hospitality heritage. It ranked right up there with "please" and "thank you," in terms of how often and how automatically you offered it, and how sincerely you meant it.

I learned it so well that, even as I enter the seventh decade of my life, I can hardly visit anyone or entertain guests without giving them something. In fact, I think my desire to gift people has increased the older I get.

I once had a neighbor call me on it. Whenever I visited her, I brought her vegetables from my garden or bread that I had baked or something of that nature. One day she just asked me point blank, "Why do you feel like you have to always bring something with you when you visit? If you just bring yourself, that's enough."

I understood her point, and she was right: I didn't *have* to bring anything in order for her to welcome me, or for us to enjoy each

147

other's company. But my motivation for gifting her so often was not about approval or self-worth. It was about love and gratitude.

"I know I don't *have* to bring anything when I come over," I responded. "But I always *want* to, because I love our friendship and I'm grateful to have you as a neighbor. It makes me feel so rich that I have to share my abundance with you!"

"Gift" comes from the PIE root *ghabh-*, which means, "to give or receive. The basic sense of the root probably is 'to hold,' which can be either in offering or in taking."

Because the indigenous practice of gifting is a natural component of interdependency and belonging, their etymologies and nuances are reviewed here again. "Belong" comes from the PIE root meaning "long, extended." To belong is to be pertinent, and "pertain" comes from the French word meaning "to hold." "Inter-depend" comes from PIE root words that describe a stretching and hitching connection between and among entities or parties.

Collectively these words present a picture of long-stretching connections that hold the whole in place, allowing for back-and-forth actions of giving and receiving. This is the picture of indebtedness, which is the feature that makes the practice of belonging and inter-depending successful. If indebtedness is the necessary condition for interdependency and belonging, then gifting is the currency.

What does it mean to "gift?" Gifting involves giving one's own possession to another in a way that honors both parties as well as the gift, with no expectation of reciprocity or compensation. Not once did my neighbor match my gift-giving with her own before I left her house, nor did she repay me in some way for the gift I gave her. However, several times during our brief time as neighbors, she did give me some beautiful handmade gifts that she made for me. Like my gifts to her, these were given in love and gratitude.

In the most indigenous sense, gifting involves a mutual understanding that "ownership" is not a personal or individual quality, but a village-wide quality. In a gifting community, everyone gifts and everyone receives, regularly and consistently. More often than not, giving and receiving are ceremonially conducted. "Potlatch" is the most common example of such ceremony, where a village-wide feast is held and all in the village engage in gift-giving. Those who are considered to be the wealthiest are the ones who give the most away. There is prestige given to those who give the most of their possessions to others.

Another feature of indigenous-minded gifting is often misunderstood as insincerity, and has led to the phrase "Indian Giver" being hurled as an insult. Jamie Sams clarifies the true meaning of Indian Giving:

> The concept of Indian Giving has been misunderstood for a long time. Our Native American Ancestors taught us that every living thing and inanimate object in our world has a mission. Whether it be a sweater, a cook pot, a lodge, a stone, or a tree. When a gift is given to another, the person receiving that gift must understand the gift's mission. The use of the object given determines its purpose. If the recipient does not use the gift, the purpose and mission of service contained in that object is dishonored. When this occurs, the giver has the right to reclaim the gift, giving it to another person who needs it or will use it. Then the usefulness of the object will serve its purpose and be able to complete its mission. If a person has many blankets and another person has none, it is perfectly all right to take the unused blanket back and give it to someone who needs it. In this way, the blanket's gift, of bringing warmth, is honored as having been useful to humankind.[62]

What is *not* gifting? What is *not* involved? Gifting does not involve sacrifice, because in the gift-giving economy no one is left out. All are recipients of gifts at some point. No one goes lacking while others have plenty, and no one has plenty at the expense of those who lack.

Gifting is neither a loan, nor a trade or barter; and a gift is not something that someone wants to get rid of anyway. A gift is something that has meaning and value to the giver, but also brings honor to the giver, receiver, and gift simultaneously.

Gifting is a ceremonial pleasure that feeds the perpetual give-and-receive cycle. Built into a gift economy is the practice of giving one's wealth away to make the whole village succeed. The gift economy is inclusive rather than exclusive; it favors interdependence over independence; and it promotes cooperation over competition. Perhaps gifting is the way to begin reshaping our economic model. Perhaps it is the first step toward enhancing our connectedness and belonging, and the realization of our interdependence.

Let it be, then! Let gifting be the celebration of these indigenous practices that demonstrate abundance and make us One.

Reflect

1. Reflect on a time where you thought someone's gift to you was too much. What made you think that?
2. Reflect on a time where a special gift that you gave to someone seemed underappreciated, or even unappreciated. If you had known ahead of time that the recipient was going to respond that way, would you have done anything differently? Why or why not?
3. What were you taught about owning and sharing? Do you consider your possessions to be communal property ("What's yours is mine, and vice versa."), or personal property ("What's mine is mine, and what's yours is yours.")?

4. Have you ever had an "Indian Giver" experience? What happened, and how did it make you feel?

Practice

1. Assess your own gift-giving patterns to see if they meet the indigenous qualities of gifting. For example, do you tend to give gift cards as presents rather than buying or making gifts that have more personal meaning to the recipient?

2. Don't limit your gifting to birthdays, holidays, or other special occasions. When you see something around your home or in the marketplace that makes you think, "Oh, I know who would just love that!", consider giving them that gift, just because. (This is what my mother and her mother called "a *now* present.")

3. If you're considering "re-gifting" someone (i.e., gifting someone with a gift that was originally given to you), use discernment. If it is something that you think they are in need of or would really like, it would probably qualify as gifting in the indigenous sense. But if you have no reason to believe this person needs or wants this item, then it would probably not carry the spirit of gifting.

4. Receive gifts graciously and joyfully. Accept yourself as worthy of receiving gifts for whatever reason.

5. Host a Potlatch event. (NOTE: A white elephant or gag gift exchange is the antithesis of true potlatch!)

6. Celebrate your successful practices.

7. Repeat as needed.

27

CARRY

Just because you don't <u>understand</u> Everything,
doesn't mean you can't <u>hold</u> Everything in your hands.

—Nicolas Chiviliu Tacaxoy

When I was a senior in high school, I participated in a required six-week course designed to give us experience in making decisions that we would have to make as adults. It was family-focused, so we paired up and had a mock wedding for the whole class. And then we had to proceed as couples with jobs and apartments and bills to pay . . . and then newborns.

As part of our parenthood, we had to make sure the baby was tended to, all day and every day, as in real life. That meant that unless we had the resources to secure a babysitter, we had to carry the baby with us everywhere we went—to class, to basketball practice, to the bathroom, to the movies, to bed. Our "babies" were 10-lb. bags of flour. Luckily, they fit in our backpacks, but like real babies, they seemed to gain weight over the six-week period. In fulfilling our married-with-children responsibilities, we learned that there is a lot of carrying to do if we wanted life to continue.

"Carry" comes from the Anglo-French word *carier* ("to transport in a vehicle"), and the Latin word *carrum*. "Carry," "car," and "current" all share the same PIE root, **kers-*, which means, "to run." All three terms indicate movement, and share a common function of moving something or someone from one place to another.

"Current" offers an intriguing contribution to our exploration of the indigenous meaning of "carry." When we think of an electrical current or a water current in a stream, what we visualize is their constant and consistent movement. A current appears to sustain itself as it carries an electric charge or a water molecule. If the current *is* self-sustaining, then the very least we know is that in order for anything to continue, the carrying that takes place must be steady and uninterrupted. If the current *is not* self-sustaining, then we also know that even the things that we assumed progressed on their own need to be carried. The familiar question re-emerges: "What will you do to make life continue?" Life won't continue on its own. It must be carried.

The opening quote is attributed to a Mayan shaman. The Maya are tuned in to the vitality and interrelatedness of everything in existence. Like you and me, they may not understand how each detail in the whole web of life works, but they know that each detail is needed as a vital component in the whole operation. They so recognize and accept this reality that their every word and deed is performed toward the collective goal of keeping life going.

The Maya perform their daily tasks to help the sun to rise, the plants to grow, the water to flow, and the stars to come out at night. Our Westernized minds perceive these natural events to be automatic and outside of any human influence or responsibility, but the Maya know better. They don't watch the day begin like most of us; they carry it into being. They arise from their beds as Father Sun rises from his, and for the rest of the day the people and the sun are comrades, working cooperatively to keep the day going and the sun moving across the sky. Where the consequence of not going to work in the modern Westernized culture is not getting paid, the same scenario in the village would mean the sun might not come up.

Carrying is a tediously daily enterprise; yet it is a timeless one, connecting past, present, and future together in each moment. Every day, we carry. All of us around the world, we carry so many things to keep life going: groceries, firewood, children, tools, laundry. Every day, we labor to keep our lives going, because if we didn't, something would stop. In other words, our refusal to carry would mean that the future would never come into being.

Our forebears knew this to be true, and that's why they carried us. We are the present day legacy of our ancestors who accepted the responsibility of carrying life forward; and we are the present day promise of the continuity of life for our children and grandchildren, the future carriers of life. Thanks to our ancestral heritage, and our indigenous souls, we can find reassurance in knowing that we are needed to help the sun rise every day. We can realize ourselves in good, great company as we remember that we join millions of people around the world when we're washing dirty dishes after an evening meal. And together, at our respective sinks, we are all tucking Father Sun into his western horizon bed with our various lullabies, all ending in some form of, "See you tomorrow, when we do all this again."

Reflect

1. Reflect on who has carried you, literally and figuratively, over the course of your lifetime, and how it has shaped you as a person.
2. Now reflect on who and what you have carried. What did it mean to you then, and what does it mean to you now?

Practice

1. Besides laundry and babies and briefcases, who and what shall you carry on a daily basis? Here is a non-exhaustive list:
    *   gratitude and humility for the miracle of our lives, and the carrying that others performed to make us possible;
    *   a persistent curiosity about who we are, where we came from, and why we're here;
    *   a practical and reverent respect for the life/death cycle, and the joy and grief that it generates;
    *   wisdom to distinguish between what to carry and what not to carry;
    *   courage to believe that we are enough, sufficient to the task; that we are fully capable of such life-continuing carrying;
    *   dreams that manifest into future generations of all living things;
    *   memories of loved ones whose lives have ended but whose legacies remain;
    *   love, forgiveness, and honor for what we know as well as what we don't know;
    *   someone whose path is too difficult or load is too heavy for them to manage by themselves;
    *   our ancestors and spirit guides, and other unseen forces of beneficence;
    *   Mother Earth, the living Gaia, as she continues to heal and return to her natural 5th-Dimension home; and
    *   our fully-human selves, in a manner in which our ancestors and our grandchildren would be proud.
2. Celebrate your successful practices.
3. Repeat as needed.

28

HONOR

Our ancestors are watching.

−Martin Prechtel

The previous chapter focused on what, who, and how to carry in order for life to continue. This chapter emphasizes the regard we have for the precious load that we carry.

The word "honor" comes from the Old French word *honorer*, meaning, "respect, esteem, revere; welcome." "Respect" and "revere" both begin with *re-*, which means, "back to the original place; again, anew, once more." "Scope" and *−spect* ("look at") share the same PIE root, **spek-*, which means, "to observe." *-vere* comes from the Latin word *vereri*, meaning, "stand in awe of, fear, respect." Its original PIE root **wer-* means, "to be or become aware of, perceive, watch out for" in a protecting way.

Collectively, these terms indicate that to "honor" someone or something is to once again or in a new way, observe with awe, and watch over with intent to protect. Let's look at each of these definitional components.

In order to look at something again or in a new way, we must entertain different points of view. To do so is to reject the lazy way of seeing that keeps us safely in our comfort zones, unchallenged. Instead, we are asked to consider (which literally means "survey on all sides") different meanings of what we see when we're willing to literally or figuratively move around to take in other points of view.

The most immediate place we can start is with ourselves. An old Serbian Proverb urges us to see ourselves in a new way: "Be humble, for you are made of the earth. Be noble, for you are made of stars." If we are willing to do this for ourselves, we are on the way to likewise honor others. We are all sparks of the whole Source of life, no matter how much we may irritate or oppose each other. "Namaste" is the Hindu greeting that essentially says, "The divine in me acknowledges the divine in you."

Next, what observations are we making about our daily routines and interactions? Are there ways that we can see anew that can lead us to honor our workplaces, schools, houses of worship, and other communal settings more? Do we see the world as a cruel, threatening place, or as a life-affirming, friendly one?

If we're willing to see in a new way, we will discover what Robert Benson proclaims: "All of the places of our lives are sanctuaries. Some of them just happen to have steeples. And all of the people in our lives are saints. It's just that some of them have day jobs, and most will never have feast days named for them."[63]

An equally needed shift in perspective pertains to planet Earth. All of Mother Earth is alive. None of our planet's manifestations are inanimate. Gaia is the term used to describe Earth as a living, breathing organism. Fortunately, the percentage of people on the planet who are embracing this reality continues to grow, seeing Earth not as merely a one-stop resource shop but as a Mother who calls us her own.

Similarly, perhaps now more than ever, we are called to observe anew the reciprocal relationship between the seen (physical) and unseen (spiritual, energetic) realms. The spirit beings depend on us to demonstrate how one can live spiritually in a physical body, something the spirits cannot do; and we depend on them for spiritual guidance in a physical world. Our ancestors and spirit guides are watching us; are we honoring them?

The second component of honoring is awe, which means, "fear, terror, great reverence." It comes from the PIE root *agh- ("to be depressed, be afraid"). From this same root comes a relative of "awe," the verb "ail," which means, "to be troublesome, painful." To observe with awe means to open oneself up to the vulnerability required to let in something new, something potentially life-changing. While the experience may not be one of sheer terror, it is one that will shake the ground under our feet.

Observing with awe requires us to get out of our routine way of seeing and being in the world, and to let our guard down to allow something or someone to move us deeply and change us dramatically. It can be scary to witness that kind of life-changing power that comes from somewhere else other than ourselves, and to be at its mercy. Observing with awe asks us to stop in our tracks, feel our eyes swell with tears, and say, "Wow!"

The third and final component of honoring is to watch over in a protective way. With our honoring, we preserve the relationship between the object and us. The more we are able to see anew the aspects of our lives, the more awed we become, and the more we desire to sustain our deepened connections.

For example, one of the most profound changes of my life has been the remembering of my ancestors. This was not something I could have done on my own, because my Westernized amnesia was so severe. My shaman teachers had to remind me about the powerful role my ancestors play. My ancestors are ever-present. My ancestors brought me to this world they helped build. They are the guides and supervisors in the spirit world to which the physical world yields.

The more space and time I dedicated to considering my ancestors, the more in awe I became. "Now I feel them all around me, all the time," I explained to a friend and colleague, "and I'll never, ever feel alone again."

To protect and preserve the relationship, I honor my ancestors several times each day with a small portion of each of my meals, and a short prayer of gratitude: "Thank you, ancestors, for bringing me here. May I be worthy of coming from you, and may I become an ancestor worth coming from."

For honoring, humans commonly use an altar. Altars range from simple to extravagant and ornate, and their variations correspond to the diversity of humans who construct them. Their basic purpose has remained the same throughout humanity's existence: to reconnect (re-member) us to the Holies, the ancestors, and the dead.

Altars are the feeding table for the honorees, and the food consists of actual food as well as candles, incense, flowers, presents, or other items that embody the relationship between the seen and the unseen, and the living and the dead. Figurines and photographs are common. Praying, singing, and the telling of stories at the altar also feed the honorees.

Of importance is calling our ancestors, the dead, and spirit guides by name and talking to them like they are fully present—because they are! The altar is the dedicated site honoring the ever-presence of the unseen, and indeed the rendezvous spot for them and us to watch over and protect our connections on a regular basis. Entry into this sacred space commands the full honoring process each and every time.

Some people have one substantial altar in their home; others have smaller ones located throughout the house. And of course there are outdoor altars all over the world, from gravesites, labyrinths and fire pits to ancient landmarks honoring energy vortexes and defining events in spiritual or religious history.

Along with the altars in our homes, these outdoor altars and sacred sites must be approached and addressed with great respect. And just as the altars in our homes are not trophy cases or mini-galleries, sacred outdoor sites are not to be reduced to tourist attractions for photo opportunities. Altars are alive, and anytime we approach one, we need to do so as if we're reconnecting ourselves to something or someone special to us.

Altars also demarcate the sacred place where ritual can be performed, and the next chapter is devoted to this important practice.

Reflect

To honor is to see in a new way, in awe, and to watch over protectively.

1. Reflect on how you honor:
   - Yourself.
   - Other humans.
   - Mother Earth and all of her non-human life forms.
   - The spirit realm (e.g., ancestors, spirit guides, etc.).
2. Reflect on these common uses of the word "honor." Is the three-part definition of "honor" apparent in these examples?
   - "On my honor, I do solemnly swear . . . ."
   - "It is an honor for me to . . . ."
   - "I will honor your request . . . ."
   - "Your Honor, may I approach the bench?"

Practice

1. Construct an altar in or outside of your home.
   - Select thoughtfully the items you place on it, such that each item has a purpose for being there. You may want to include some of the items suggested in the chapter; but also think about what unique objects you have that would deepen the connection between you and your honorees.
   - Make a daily practice of visiting the altar to honor who and what the altar has been prepared for.

- In determining what to say or do at the altar, treat the visit as a special conversation between you and the ones you're honoring and remembering. It could be as simple as, "I light a candle in memory of you today, and I will carry the flame of our connection with me when I go." Chapters 21 (Bless) and 29 (Rite) provide additional guidance for what to do and say at your altar.
- At least on a seasonal basis, change the arrangement and items on the altar, to refresh it. Both you and your honorees will feel rejuvenated by it.

2. Celebrate your successful practices.
3. Repeat as needed.

29

RITE

So teach us to number our days, that we may
apply our hearts unto wisdom.

—Psalm 90:12

The necessity for humans to perform ritual is so real and unavoidable, the noun, "rite" is proposed here as a verb. If we don't have rituals to perform, it's our human obligation and need to create them, for the mutual benefit of the seen and unseen worlds. Ritual is both a responsibility and a necessity, to acknowledge and feed the interdependent relationship we have with the Spirit realm.

"Ritual" comes from the word "rite," which originates from the PIE root *re(i)-* ("to count, number"). The word "arithmetic" comes from this same root. The word "read" is related in origin, thus expanding the meaning of "rite" to include "to reason; to succeed, accomplish; to take thought, attend to; to deliberate, consider; to counsel, advise." These meanings speak to several aspects of what ritual is, what it accomplishes, and why it is so powerful.

Rituals are very intentional and deliberate practices that succeed in marking the most significant events in the days of our lives, many of which we share with all of humanity: birthday, community/ village membership (e.g., naming ceremony, baptism, communion), initiation, graduation, marriage/divorce, parenthood, retirement/ elderhood, and death. The numbering aspect is seen not only in the chronology of these milestones in any given life, but also in maintaining the count of those *preceding* us, whose roll call now *includes* us. And the count will continue with the generations to come. In this way, the performance of ritual both counts and perpetuates life.

Ritual is humanity's way of making sure life goes on. Having children won't accomplish it alone; it requires the sacred act of adding the children's lives and their passages to the ancestral count. What parents wouldn't want this? What parents would willfully arrest this ancient, world-turning, life-sanctifying process?

As one would expect, the root meanings of ritual reveal the degree of attention and dedication required to do ritual right. While a ritual doesn't have to be elaborate or lengthy, it does have to be completely intentional. It is neither a casual enterprise, nor a routine or habit. No two rituals are identical, because the Spirit is involved. Done well and honorably, ritual creates the space for the Divine to enter in. It summons the Holies to attend, and relinquishes control to them. A true ritual is a yielding and vulnerable human practice.

Because every ritual experience is unique to the situation and the people involved, the effect upon and the response of the Spirit will be different every time. The Divine doesn't do re-runs. African shaman Malidoma Somé describes the spiritual component of ritual this way:

> Ritual is the gathering with others in order to feel
> Spirit's call, to express spontaneously and publicly
> whatever emotion needs to be expressed, to create,
> in concert with others, an unrehearsed and deeply
> moving response to Spirit, and to feel the presence of
> the community, including the ancestors, throughout
> the experience. It is a dance with Spirit, the soul's

way of interacting with the Other world, the human psyche's opportunity to develop a relationship with the symbols of this world and the Spirits of the Other.[64]

Relational ritual unites human and holy beings in a common effort, to manifest transformation. The "attending to" arrow points both ways: ritual requires *both* parties to arrive with their best selves. The Divine will always do so; we humans had better do so as well. Ritual is one of the most organic *and* transcendent acts we can perform to make meaning of our lives, and to acknowledge the Divine and our longing for it in our lives.

In great company of the Holies and all humans past, present, and future, we count and account for our lives, invoking Divine presence and guidance, offering bent-knee praise and bowed-head gratitude. In ritual we join with those standing right next to us, and also with those who are ten or two-thousand miles away at this moment. We join with our ancestors whose name we bear and facial characteristics we wear; and with those yet unborn. Collectively, we act out our will that life go on, and that the balance of our lives and our communities be restored and blessed. Together, we acknowledge the cycle of life and death and where we are in it, discerning our own footsteps on the path our forebears made, and smoothing it out a bit more for the feet of our children and grandchildren.

When is a ritual needed? Most rituals fall under one of these M's:

- **Milestones Rituals** – These rituals are rites of passage for individuals or groups in transition. These include rituals celebrating births, child dedications, and initiations into adulthood. They also mark graduations, weddings, retirement, reaching elderhood, and death.

- **Mending Rituals** – These rituals repair the broken or damaged psyche or spirit. Someone suffering from addiction or trauma might benefit from such a ritual. Mending rituals also provide physical healing of an individual, group, or even the Earth. World Water Day or Earth Day celebrations are examples of mending rituals for our Earth.

- **Moment Rituals** – These rituals are designed for sudden crisis situations that disrupt daily life such as a natural or human-made disaster or an unexpected loss.

- **Maintenance Rituals** – These rituals preserve the ongoing health and wholeness of a relationship. Anniversary celebrations are maintenance rituals. When we shore up a community to resist the normal wear and tear of life with a seasonal or cyclical celebration, that is a maintenance ritual.

A proper ritual requires these particular components:

- **Intent** – There should be a specific purpose for the ritual, and it needs to be stated in the preparation for the ritual as well as during the ritual.

- **Story** – What is the particular meaning behind this ritual? What is the human context, including the culturally-specific and also the universal?

- **Community** – Who are the people participating in the ritual, and why is it important to this particular group? A ritual can be as small as one-to-one, but more often it involves a group. It is also important to note that all people in attendance must participate. Rituals are not spectator events; they require the participation of everyone who is present. Further, participants must enter into the ritual with respect for what is about to happen, humility in the face of the upcoming communion with the Holies, and the willingness to relinquish control of the outcome of the ritual. This doesn't mean the ritual itself cannot be planned; rather, it means there should be no specific expectations about how the Spirit realm will respond, influence, or transform.

- **Appropriate Space** – The ritual space must be intentionally selected and prepared, such that it enhances the participants' likelihood of being transformed during the ritual. The setting should be free of distractions or interruptions, and needs to accommodate well the participants (e.g. age differences, people with disabilities, etc.), materials (see symbols and elements), and actions to take place. The ideal location would be outdoors in a natural setting, but sometimes this is not possible. When this is the case, then natural elements can be brought indoors.

- **Symbols and Elements** – Candles, plants, water, feathers, rocks, seashells, seeds, and other such meaningful objects are important for the human participants and the Divine that the ritual invokes. Whatever symbols are used, the goal is to illustrate the connection between the participants, the physical plane they are in, and the Spiritual realm.

- **Action** – What steps, gestures, music, or other activities are involved and why? How does each action cohere with the overall intent of the ritual?

- **Prayer and invocation** – This is the most important and most necessary component of ritual, yet the most commonly left out. Performing ritual without the presence of the Divine is like making bread without a leavening agent. A ritual without the Holies present is not a ritual, it's a tradition or party or a celebration or a support group . . . potentially anything *but* a ritual. If ideas for rituals do not include a definitive prayer or invocation, make sure to add this critical component.

A hymn in the Unitarian Universalist hymnal is entitled, "For All That Is Our Life."[65] Each verse offers an occasion for ritual: "For the gift of life, which we are called to use to build the common good; for services and love we give and receive; for sorrow, failure, pain, fear, or loss that we bear; for our glad days filled with work, rest and love."

We need ritual for all that is our life, so that we may apply our hearts in our numbered days.

Reflect

1. Is ritual a regular part of your life? If so, describe some examples. If not, is ritual something you now want to make room for in your life?
2. Looking over the four types of ritual (the four M's), reflect on examples you've experienced in each of these categories.
3. What circumstances in your life right now are ripe for ritual?

Practice

1. Choose one of the circumstances you identified in the 3rd Reflection above.
2. Using the list of ritual components from the chapter, create a ritual that is tailored to your circumstance. If you've never done this before, start small and keep it simple. After you gain more confidence and experience in designing and leading rituals, feel free to create more elaborate ones.
3. Sometimes a ritual performed by yourself is fitting, but ideally, ritual is a communal event. Invite others to help you plan and set up the ritual, and to participate in it.
4. Consider using the altar you created (previous chapter) for your ritual. At the very least, let your altar-building experience be a starting point for collecting what you will need for the ritual.

5. Begin and end your ritual with clear purpose and direction (e.g., "We gather here today to . . ." at the beginning; and "We close with . . ." and "As we depart . . ." at the end).

6. Research and collect rituals that others have created, and modify them as needed for your particular situations.

7. Celebrate your successful practices.

8. Repeat as needed.

30

ELDER

An Elder is an ancestor in training.

–Malidoma Some´

For more than a decade, I was the chaplain at a pediatric long-term care facility, where the young residents were medically fragile and reliant on 24-hour skilled nursing care. Just months into the job, there was an infant death that took us all by surprise. During those first few hours of rendering pastoral care to the staff and family, I realized that something else was needed that I could not provide, because I wasn't a parent myself. When I had the opportunity, I went to my office and called my 70-year old mother. When she answered, I choked up right away, but I managed to speak.

"I need a Mommie prayer," I requested.

"A Mommie prayer?" she asked.

"Yes. A baby died here today, and I've said all kinds of prayers. But the mother of this baby also needs a prayer from another mother."

"Of course. Yes. Tell me the mother's name, and the baby's name, and I'll say a prayer after we hang up. And then I'll gather a couple of my dear friends here who have helped me out with prayer before, and together we'll pray some more for mother and baby, okay?"

"Yes," I sniffled, "that would be wonderful."

After a moment of silence, my mother said, "I can't imagine what it would be like for one of my children to die. I don't know where I'd find the strength to go on."

"In the prayers sent by other Elder Mommies," I replied. "That's where you'd find it."

The word "elder" comes from the Old English word *eldra* ("older person, parent; ancestor; chief, prince"), which comes from the Latin word *alere* ("to feed, nourish, suckle, bring up, increase"). The PIE root of "elder" is *sen-*, from which the words "senior" and "senile" come, both of which mean "old."

However, another meaning associated with this PIE root is "dry standing grass from the previous year," similar to the definition of Elder that shaman Malidoma Somé gives: "someone who is dry, cured, solid, lasting, and who knows something."[66] If we think that weathered, dried-out plants have no more to offer, consider the flavor and healing they add to our lives in the form of spices, herbs, and teas!

In the earliest years, the word "elder" carried no negative connotations with it. Any associations of weakness or infirmity attributed to "old," "senior," or "senile" came much later. This drift in definition has resulted in two distinct terms: "elderly" and "elder." The former diminishes the value of old people in society, while the latter elevates their status because of their wisdom and experience.

While the elderly are put out to pasture, or go there voluntarily, elders are acknowledged and relied upon for their unique roles in the community. From an indigenous perspective, elders are some of the most important people in the village, because they are most instrumental in making sure that life goes on.

Elders have three major roles in the community. One of them is Mentor. While parents are the major providers for their children, they are not inclined to watch their children's childhood die, through initiation into adulthood. Instead, it is the grandparents who are charged with mentoring the youth into and through the initiation process that launches them into adulthood.

Specifically, Elders are the ones who identify the young people's inborn gifts and purposes, and offer guidance accordingly. They not only praise the youth for their gifts and identities, they also challenge them with tough enough lessons and opportunities to reveal those gifts and apply them to their life purposes. Further, the elders make sure that there are venues for the public acknowledgement of the youth's accomplishments in their maturation process.

Elders are also the storytellers, the ones who tell of the legacies of past generations as they help the youth discover who and where they are genealogically, and cosmically. The contribution that Elders make in the initiation process of the youth cannot be overstated. The survival of the whole community depends on it.

The second major role of elders is Carrier. The Mommie-prayer story is an example of an Elder carrying a painful fact of life with grace and mercy: sometimes children die, and elders know the importance and power of prayer in these situations. Elders, having accumulated a wealth of personal experience and wisdom, have had lots of practice in developing their carrying skills. They've witnessed hard times, sickness and death, wrong-doings and unexpected troubles, and so they are not as easily overwhelmed by other people's grief, anger, or drama as younger adults are.

They've also learned different ways of seeing and being in the world, and therefore are able to offer insights that others haven't considered. An Elder is able to create a space to hold all kinds of lifetime events in a way that lets them breathe, settle, and ultimately reveal what they have to teach us. Elders have a "grand scheme of things" perspective, and can offer advice in that context in a way that inspires a course of action rather than dictating it.

The third major role of Elders is Bridge. With the exception of babies, Elders are the most familiar with the Other world, the spiritual realm. Newborns just arrived from there; Elders are preparing to return there. That's one reason why grandparents and babies are so infatuated with each other!

In anticipation of their final days, Elders devote much of their attention to the interaction between the spirit realm and the physical realm, and are recognized by the village as living bridges between the two worlds. They are like ambassadors to the spirit realm, always with the goal of nurturing the relationship between the community and the spirits, ancestors, and the dead. It is the Elders' knowledge of the spirit world and its relationship to the physical world that is so critical. Elders take this role seriously, and are often the spiritual leaders in the community. Where indigenous practices are still common, it is the elders who maintain the shrines and make sure that rituals are being performed dutifully and frequently. Remnants of this practice exist in our current houses of worship, as much of the work in church communities is often carried out and/or led by the Elders.

The common thread in all three of these roles is the balance that the Elders promote and strive to maintain in the interconnected web that is the village. All three roles work toward nurturing relationships among people, other living beings, the earthly and celestial bodies, and the Other world where spirit guides, ancestors, and the dead reside. Elders have the responsibility of identifying and addressing any imbalance in the community, and inspiring the village to respond accordingly. Wherever Elders are honored, their leadership and wisdom are cherished and their advice is followed.

Ancestors perform in the Other world as Elders do in this one. As ancestors in training, Elders are legacy builders. Through mentoring, carrying, and bridging, Elders leave their enduring mark on the community that will outlive them. Their influence continues after they die, as they transition from Elder to Ancestor. Let us honor our Elders while they are here, and model what we learn from them as we endeavor to become Elders ourselves.

The final role for Elders is their transition from one who feeds to one who becomes the food. Our Elders are our teachers about death, which is the focus of the next chapter.

Reflect

1. Reflect on the distinction between "elderly" and "Elder." Which one are you/do you want to be?
2. Who are the Elders in your life; and how have they mentored, carried, and bridged?

Practice

1. If you are under the age of 50, look to your Elders for mentoring, carrying, and bridging. If you don't have any, look for some, and woo them to "adopt" you.
2. If you are 50 years old or older, accept the mantle of Elder. (NOTE: There's nothing magic about the age of 50. Elderhood can begin a bit earlier or later, but think of 50 years of age as a reference point.)
3. Thank (Chapter 25) and honor (Chapter 28) your Elders often.
4. In a culture that under-appreciates and under-utilizes its Elders, commit to changing that norm, and creating opportunities for our "elderly" to practice their Elder skills and be honored for them.
5. Celebrate your successful practices.
6. Repeat as needed.

31

DIE

The attitude of the Indian toward death, the test and background of life, is entirely consistent with his character and philosophy. Death has no terror for him; he meets it with simplicity and perfect calm, seeking only an honorable end as his last gift to his family and descendants.

–Ohi'ye S'a

My cat Harrison taught me all I needed to know about dying. In the last year of his life, I watched as he got skinnier and weaker, and I knew that his death was not far off. His energy level and appetite decreased along with his ability to digest food. And then one day he and I both knew the instant that he began his dying process.

I remember the breakfast he had, scant as it was, and where he sat to wash his face and paws after eating. No sooner had he finished this grooming when he regurgitated everything he had just eaten, and then some. For a silent moment, we both stared at the puddle and pile on the rug, and it was instantly clear to both of us that he had just eaten his last meal.

For the next several days he got weaker by the hour, yet increasingly unsettled. He roamed the house looking for something or someone that wasn't food, or water, or me. His eyes stopped focusing on objects before him, and he never made eye contact with me again until moments before his death. We both agonized as he limped and dragged himself around in utter dissatisfaction and confusion, and I futilely tried to help him find peace.

Toward the end of the third day of this process, he finally calmed enough to stay curled up in his bed, as long as he could see and feel my presence very nearby. For a few quiet, love-soaked, peace-filled moments, we rested in the companionship we had shared for more than 17 years. And then he lifted his weary body out of his bed, pulled himself into the back corner of the closet, and he died.

The PIE root of "die" is *dheu-*, meaning, "to pass away, die, become senseless." The phrase "to pass away" is often used to mask our discomfort with saying the word "die," so the etymology of these words offers yet more information. "Pass" comes from the Vulgar Latin word *passare*, meaning, "to step, walk, pace." The word "away" is comprised of *a-* ("off of, away from"); and *way*, from the Old English word *weg* ("road, path; course of travel, space") and the PIE root *wegh-*, which means, "to move." The word "weigh" comes from this same root, and its original meanings include "lift, carry, support, sustain, bear, move."

Altogether, to "pass away" means to walk away from the course of travel, to lift off the weight of bearing or sustaining. All of this I watched Harrison do over a three-day period: He walked away from his food and water dishes; he stepped off of his well-trod familiar pathways through the house and wandered into new areas in search of the spirit realm that beckoned him; he abandoned his 3rd-Dimension senses; and finally he lifted the weight of his physical body off of his ascension-bound soul.

Harrison taught me that neither dying nor watching someone die is easy. But he also taught me how to know when death is imminent, and how to follow its lead instinctively and courageously. While my Westernized mind wanted to hustle him to the vet's office to hasten his death and spare him the discomfort of dying, my indigenous soul knew that the discomfort we were both experiencing was coming not from physical pain in his body, but from his soul (spirit) trying to wrestle itself free of his failing body. My indigenous soul knew the importance of bearing witness to that holy process, simultaneously grieving *and* blessing him on his way, and knowing that as he was desperately seeking his loved ones from the other side, they were in fact lining up to meet him as he crossed over.

The advantage of having one's pet be a death teacher is that the whole trajectory can take place in the home, not in a hospital or nursing facility. My indigenous soul remembers how natural the process is of allowing death to take its course, and to set its stage in one's own home with loved ones around to support, grieve, and bless. My Westernized mind knows how atypical that is in most modern homes. The opportunity to bear witness to someone's dying is neither standard nor desired in contemporary society.

How we die is largely determined by our own understanding of what death is. Our indigenous souls know what death is, and can distinguish it from what death isn't. Here is a summary of those contrasts:

- Death is a natural part of the life cycle, and as such, it is a birthright. One's death is to be honored and celebrated with as much fervor as one's birth. Death is neither the opposite of life, nor the end of it. It is a transition of the everlasting soul to its original Dimension, and the physical transition of the body into dirt, dust, and ash that is the soil from which new life germinates. In this regard, death is also a responsibility, an obligation to future life. Death does not ask us to sacrifice, it asks us to gift the next generation. It asks us to make that final step, from feeding to becoming the food.

- Death is an active process, not a passive one. Death isn't done to us; it is something we engage in, like a dance or a wrestling match. In his CD set, *Angel or Executioner*[67] and his book,

Die Wise,[68] Stephen Jenkinson describes thoroughly and elaborately the partnering aspect we have with our deaths.

- Like birth, death is a spiritual and physical event, not a medical event. From an indigenous standpoint, birth and death do not need to be managed or manipulated. They need to be allowed to unfold naturally, in their own time and place, midwifed by love, awe, and honor. Consider that discomfort is a feature of birth and death that is meant to be carried, not necessarily a complication to be managed, as the story of Harrison illustrates. Our births were uncomfortable, and the chances are good that our deaths will involve struggle as well; but attempts to treat that struggle as a medical complication hamper the soul's journey into and back out of this earthly realm. (NOTE: "Pain" and "discomfort" are not the same thing. Therefore, the treatment of chronic physical pain is compatible with a natural dying process.)

- Death is a no-judgment and no-guilt event, not a failure or a punishment. Death is the inevitable result of being alive, and needn't be blamed on how much or how little someone did to stay healthy or be a good person. "Why *me?*" is a common response to a prognosis, as if there were some people who were allowed to be spared from ever dying. Yet we would never proclaim "Why *her?*" at the birth of a baby girl. Death isn't any more unjust than birth is; both are miracles and both are gifts.

- Death is a lifelong companion to learn from, not an enemy to conquer. In her two-CD set, *The Radiant Coat*,[69] Clarissa Pinkola Estes describes death as a companion who joined us even in the womb, who helped midwife us into this life, and who will help midwife us out of our earthly bodies at the end of our lives. In between our entry and exit, death is our teacher throughout life, reminding us to honor our lives and all living things with every breath and step we take. Our indigenous souls welcome this companionship, for it provides guidance on how to live every moment with attention and intention. Further, when our time to die comes, we are familiar enough with our death that we do not fear it.

- Death is the acknowledgement that our purpose for this lifetime has been completed, and is the final stipulation in our sacred contract with the Universe. Whether our 3rd-Dimension minds realize it or not, our own deaths were something we agreed to even before we were born. Our indigenous souls know of this truth, and so it is up to us to remember. Once we are willing to accept that reality, it will be easier to shed any expectations we have about our death or the deaths of others, such as the illusion that children aren't supposed to die before their parents.

- Rather than an unwanted termination of a "bucket list," death is our initiation into our new role as ancestors. When we die, we join the esteemed ranks of ancestors, and continue the work we did as Elders, nurturing and protecting the community we once called home. Still connected and still communicating from higher Dimensions, we now serve in ways that we weren't able to as 3rd-Dimension inhabitants.

In this new age of ascension, we are called to die in the manner that honors our indigenous souls. We are called to plan for it and to carry it, all of our lives. First we need to shed the illusions surrounding death that make us strangers to and victims of it—fear, anger, guilt, judgment, independence, and more. Only then will there be room in our lives to befriend death. The sooner we do this, the better. Once we have reconciled our relationship with death in general and our own death in particular, it will serve us well in learning that the small and large initiations throughout our lives are preparation for the ultimate initiation that our own deaths will bring.

Arm in arm with our deaths, it is wise to partner with both the spirit realm and the physical realm to accommodate us in our death planning and in our dying. Inasmuch as these relationships are already rich and vibrant, they are now the resources we need for granting our death wishes.

From the spirit realm, let us ask for the wisdom to know when we have fulfilled our purposes in this world, and when we are in our last days. Let us acknowledge this final clause of our sacred contract with the cosmos, and prepare our "death song," our holy agreement to die. In our singing, let us woo the spirit realm to prepare for our homecoming, with specific requests of where and to whom we wish to return. May we call the ancestors to us, and sing so convincingly that they cannot resist the invitation to reunite with us. May the heavenly stage now be set for our transition.

As we prepare spiritually for our final days, let us also partner with the physical realm in order to secure an environment fully-suitable for such a special occasion as death. Indigenously speaking, death is a communal event. While each person's death song and path are unique, it takes a village to properly honor death and to launch the dying into ascension. As we die, we will need to be surrounded by people who will allow us to die, who will bless us on our way, and who will remember us the moment we expire and long afterwards.

As the physical and spiritual realms synchronize in accordance with our wishes, we are then called to claim our birthright, to die when it's our time. Let us be wise enough and courageous enough to say, "This is my last meal," and to respectfully decline all life-prolonging efforts.

And as we prepare to "Drop our Robes," may we embody if not speak our legacy, such as these words fashioned by Jamie Sams:

> I have earned every wrinkle on my face, and I find
> them beautiful. These wrinkles mark the paths I have
> followed and the lessons I have learned. I have used
> the curiosity of my mind to discover the truth. I have
> used the gifts of my spirit to connect to the Earth

Mother and the Creator, and I have used the fire in my heart to love without judgment. I am happy to have used all my gifts. I am content with my passage because I have given purpose to every part of my being. Now that all those things are used up, I am at peace. I have completed the vision that was given me.[70]

Reflect

1. Do you have a pet death story? How does it compare to the one about Harrison?
2. Have you been a witness to another human's dying? How has it shaped your thoughts and feelings about dying and death?
3. In what ways have you prepared for your own dying and death, and the dying and death of your loved ones?
4. How are "dying" and "death" different? From a practical standpoint, why does this difference matter?

Practice

1. If you haven't already done so, commit the time and discernment required to think about and plan for your own dying and death.
2. Record and communicate your thoughts, beliefs, and wishes about your own dying and death to your loved ones. There is a variety of tools and aids to help you with this process, and they can be found when you do research on Advance Directives. Your local hospice is also a great resource for these materials.
3. Once you've done this, now remind yourself what your purpose is for being here in this lifetime. The goal for each of us is to fulfill that purpose before we die. Now that you

are "carrying" your own death (i.e., having placed it on your own radar screen for good), revisit your life's purpose and gauge your progress in fulfilling it.

4. Imagine the deaths of your loved ones. That is, carry the reality of their deaths with you, along with your own death. As painful as this may seem ahead of time, it will prepare you to respond to their dying when it happens. It will not *spare* you from grief, but it will *prepare* you for the grieving you will do at their deaths.

5. Celebrate your successful practices.

6. Repeat as needed.

32

COORDINATE

You are every thing, every being, every emotion,
every event, every situation.
You are unity. You are infinity. You are love/light, light/love.
You are. This is the Law of One.

—Ra (Law of One)

This final chapter answers two questions that you may be asking at this point: "What do I do now?" and "Where do I go from here?"

You've been assured that you've got everything you need within you to operate at your full capacity (be fully human), and you've read and reflected upon a variety of suggested practices that will help you do just that. Yet, you may be feeling overwhelmed with all that has been presented, and perhaps are having a hard time determining how and where to start putting these practices into action. The Practice section of this chapter will guide you in getting started.

As for the second question—"Where do I go from here?"—this chapter orients you by addressing where in the universe you currently are. Being fully human requires an ongoing process of coordination. Not only do you have everything you need *inside* of you to be fully human, you also have everything you need *outside* of you. The indigenous soul within you is inextricably bound to and interacts with all that is outside of you. Use this chapter, along with the Appendix, to help you to remember the coordinates within and around you that let you to operate at your full capacity.

The verb "coordinate" comes from the Latin *coordinare*, meaning, "to place in the same rank." Later meanings include "to arrange in proper position," and "to work together in order." It is made up of *com-* ("together") and *ordinatio* ("arrangement"), which comes from *ordo* ("row, rank, series, arrangement"). The Italic root **ord-* ("to arrange, arrangement") is where *ordo* comes from, and is also the source of *ordiri* ("to begin to weave"), which originally meant "a row of threads in a loom." Coordination deals with space and function, indicating that non–random parts or components are fit together toward the maximal function or expression of the whole.

This chapter and the Appendix offer descriptions and diagrams of some of the many coordinates that the entire cosmos and we humans share. Collectively they say, "You are *here*," like a shopping mall directory that indicates where you currently stand among all its stores. The knowledge about our intimate, energetic connections with the cosmos is ancient, and relevant. The modernized Western mind has forgotten its innate capacity to think and dwell "outside the box" of 3rd-Dimension, illusionary existence. Remember that the distinctive feature of the new age into which we have recently entered is the golden opportunity it presents for personal and planetary ascension. This age invites us to recover our innate (i.e., indigenous) ability to be multidimensionally human.

The first coordinates we'll look at are the ones within our bodies that are aligned with the universe. There are numerous models of how the human body's structure and function mirror aspects of how the universe works. Models include Leonardo DaVinci's Virtuvian Man, as well as the Tree of Life, the chakra system, and even the Caduceus and Ouroboros symbols. The universe-mirroring coordinates within our bodies described here, and illustrated in Appendix A, come from the Maya tradition.

The Cholq'ij (a.k.a. Tzolkin) calendar, previously mentioned in Chapter 7, is one of 20 calendars used by the Maya to track cycles of days, years, and celestial bodies to discern the meaning of life events, including future predictions. The mathematics of this Sacred Calendar align with the human body:

- The year is a 260-day cycle, which corresponds with the gestation period of a human fetus.

- The 260-day year is divided into 13 months, which corresponds to the 13 Uxkanel (major joints). These Uxkanel, along with the seven Ukux (chakras), are the major energetic convergence points in the body. These seven energetic points in the body vary according to vibration rates. On the far right side of the illustration in Appendix A, these seven centers (also known as chakras) are labeled "Densities," based on the varying rates of vibration from head to toe. The higher the energetic center is located in the body, the higher the rate of vibration, and the less density there is. These are the necessary conditions for ascension: high vibration, low density.

- Each of the 13 months is 20 days long, which corresponds to the 20 digits (fingers and toes) in the human body that are like receptor sites for incoming cosmic (atmospheric or heavenly) and telluric (earthly or underworld) energies. (These energies also enter us through our crown, as illustrated in Appendix A.) Denise Barrios and Denise De Peña describe the significant relationship between 20 and 13 this way:[71]

  Each of the 20 days has a distinct energy (*Nawal*), and they combine with other energies known as Powers, which run from one to 13. In this way, the energies of each day are formed by the confluence of the

energy of Power and the energy of a *Nawal*, and this
is what determines the strength and the character of
the energy that each of the 260 days of the Cholq'ij
will display (p. 3).

- The right and left sides of the body reflect the polarities that naturally exist throughout the cosmos. The right side expresses the 10 masculine, even-numbered energies, and the left side the 10 feminine, odd-numbered, energies.

- The four planes of the body that cooperate as a unit are the physical, mental, emotional, and spiritual planes. In the lower left corner of the illustration in Appendix A, these planes are labeled "Dimensions," because they represent the body's coordinates that align with the 3rd-5th Dimensions.

- Balance is the goal regarding the sides and planes of the body. If there is an imbalance between energetic polarities or in any of the planes in which we express our humanness, the risk of illness or accidents increases (see Chapter 23).

Because the Cholq'ij calendar demonstrates the intimate relationship between the human body and the cosmos it inhabits, the Maya people rely on it to guide every aspect of their individual and communal lives. The rhythms that the human body and the cosmos share make this calendar a map of destiny. If we choose to become intimately familiar with the energies of each day and how we may live in balance with them; we can coordinate our own destinies.

How are Dimensions and Densities interrelated? In the context of the great ascension that Earth and her inhabitants are currently experiencing, the terms "Dimension" and "Density" are often used interchangeably because of how closely related they are. The easiest way that I have found to distinguish them is to think of "Dimension" as *location* (i.e. *space* or *medium* rather than *place*); and "Density" as *vibration*. Let's look at each more closely.

According to Suzan Carroll, "'Dimensions' are a means of organizing different planes of existence according to their vibratory rate. Each dimension has certain sets of laws and principles that are specific to the frequency of that dimension."[72]

Based on her definition, "Dimension" is the location that hosts a certain vibration or Density level. Each Dimension, then, offers a unique environment for a specific vibratory level. (The relationship between Dimension and Density is illustrated in Appendices A, C, and D.)

Currently, human beings consciously function primarily in the 3rd Dimension, where time is experienced or perceived as linear, and reality is based on what our five senses perceive. It is a physical, material, and dense world. We typically have momentary conscious experiences in the 4th Dimension, and sometimes even in the 5th Dimension but this is fairly rare unless we are in a dream state.

It's hard to comprehend, in our 3rd Dimension world, how Earth or we can co-exist in different Dimensions, but it is nonetheless true. Sal Rachele shares a helpful example:

> We are living in all three of these realms (3rd–5th Dimensions and many more) simultaneously and making choices based on the dominant realm at the time of the choice. Some choices are aligned with all three dimensions, while others conflict. My goal is to always align these three realms when I make decisions. If I join an organization that helps feed people, for instance, I might do so on a 3rd Dimension level because I don't want to see people suffer. I might do so on a 4th Dimension level because I feel a karmic sense of responsibility or because it feels good. I might do so on a 5th Dimension level because those starving children are aspects of my Self.[73]

The Table provided in Appendix B presents a comparison of the 3rd, 4th, and 5th Dimensions.

Now let's look more closely at Density. Everything in existence, seen or unseen, is made up of energy, and thus vibrates. The denser the being is, the lower its vibration level. Interactions between energetic beings influence their vibration levels. So the vibration level of any given being at any given time varies. Being fully human, especially in this time of planetary ascension, means striving for and maintaining higher vibration levels, so that human ascension to higher Dimensions may become possible.

The seven major chakras in the body provide the framework that enables us humans to manage our own vibration levels. Each of these seven energy centers has its unique vibration level as well. When all are vibrating at their natural levels in harmony with each other, the body is in proper balance. If one or more is out of balance, it affects the whole body's balance, causing dis-ease.

I encourage the reader to explore other resources to supplement the brief overview provided here. Basically the 1st, 2nd, and 3rd chakras (which I refer to as "below the belt" chakras) are the energy centers that focus on physical safety and security, family/tribe, and self-esteem. The 4th-7th ("above the belt") chakras are involved with love, forgiveness, will power, intuition, wisdom, and spirituality. The lower chakras help us navigate our physical world and basic relationships, while the upper chakras assist us with more esoteric matters and relationships with the unseen world. Further, in *Anatomy of the Spirit*, Carolyn Myss describes the Earth-school lessons that the chakras present to us, and the Divine Laws they symbolize.[74] These are summarized in the table below, and shown in the "Chakras, Subtle Bodies, and Auras" illustration in Appendix C.

Chakra	Lessons related to:	Divine Law
1st	Material world	All is One.
2nd	Sexuality, work, physical desire, partnership	Honor One Another.
3rd	Ego, personality, self-esteem, personal power	Honor Oneself.
4th	Love, forgiveness, compassion, emotional power	Love is Divine Power.
5th	Will, self-expression	Surrender Personal Will to Divine Will.
6th	Mind, intuition, insight, wisdom	Seek Only Truth.
7th	Spirituality	Live in the Present Moment.

While activation of the higher chakras does increase one's overall vibration level, the goal is not to try to outgrow the need for lower-chakra energies and guidance. Rather, the goal is to activate all seven, so that they remain open and fully functioning. We need all of those energies to live fully human lives. We need to be grounded (1st chakra) and connected (2nd and 3rd chakras) in order to love, surrender, seek, and be fully present in the now (4th-7th chakras).

Related to the chakras are the subtle bodies, and auras. Subtle bodies are the planes of existence identified in the Maya Coordinates (Appendix A). Auras are energies directly outside the body that correspond to the internal operations of the chakras. The size and strength of the auras reflect the health and balance of the chakras. These auras can be thought of as the bridge between the chakras and the Dimensions or planes. They are the space in which a person's vibrational density can align him with the most fitting dimension at any given moment.

Finally, what do Dimensions and Densities have to do with ascension? A look at the "Ascension Trajectory" illustration in Appendix D provides another visual representation of how Dimension and Density interact. It is important to note here: In this 2-D illustration, as Dimension increases, it appears that the direction is *upward*, creating an image of horizontal layers. Visualize it instead as 3-D, and think *outward*, like spheres. This still isn't totally accurate because Dimensions higher than 3rd Dimension cannot be visualized in 3-D! But it's still better than a 2-D model. (The same is true for the planes in Appendix A, and the auras and subtle bodies in Appendix C.)

Every human being is multi-dimensional, and lives in a multi-dimensional universe; but few of us are aware of anything outside of our 3rd-Dimension, linear time-lined, physical existence. The indigenous soul within each one of us carries greater awareness and higher consciousness than we recognize or utilize in our daily lives. In Appendix D's illustration, the "Multi-Dimensional Self" label depicts that an individual actually inhabits most all of the Dimensions at any given time, even though he is only aware of one or two. Looking back at the Table in Appendix B, we see that our primary location in the 3rd Dimension means we're not operating at our full capacity until we reach at least the 5th Dimension. There, we have a much greater awareness of the fact that our total Self (note the capital 'S') is made up of all of our lives we've ever lived, in all the Dimensions we've ever inhabited. The presence or absence of that awareness is referred to as consciousness. Suzan Caroll gives a coherent explanation of the different levels of consciousness,[75] which are shown in the illustration as well:

- "Multidimensional Consciousness" is the ability to be "conscious" of more than one dimension. To be multidimensional in our consciousness we must remember that we have within us the potential to expand our perceptual awareness to the dimensions above and below our physical plane.

- "Unconscious" means unaware of and unable to attend to internal and/or external stimuli within the inhabitants' own dimension or within another dimension. Third dimensional humans are unaware of their first dimensional, second dimensional, and fourth dimensional selves. The human unconscious is best accessed through physical body messages, introspection, dreams, and meditation.

- "Conscious" means aware of and able to attend to stimuli within the inhabitants' own dimension. The third dimensional self is conscious of what can be perceived by the five physical senses of sight, hearing, touch, taste, and smell.

- "Superconscious" is a higher order of consciousness of the fifth dimension and above in which the inhabitants are able to be aware of and attend to stimuli of their own dimension as well as all the lower dimensions. The superconscious is innately multidimensional. The third dimensional self can become "conscious" of the superconscious through meditation, prayer, and by surrendering to the enfoldment of the higher order consciousness.

As already mentioned, human beings dwell in (are aware of) the 3rd Dimension, and have limited conscious experiences in other Dimensions. The trajectory for ascension for planet Earth, and for humans as well, is into the 4th Dimension for a limited amount of time, and ultimately into the 5th Dimension. This means that the 5th Dimension would then become the new 3rd Dimension for humans, the new location in which we are fully aware, fully conscious. The 5th Dimension is a breakthrough or threshold Dimension, the level at which we become ready to explore higher Dimensions. It's like the big jump from elementary school ("I've graduated!") to the first year of middle school ("I'm starting over again!").

As the illustration in Appendix D shows, Mother Earth, the

living Gaia, is well into the 4th Dimension, and bound for the 5th Dimension at this point. She longs for us to join her!

Reflect

1. Have you ever felt an intimate connection between the universe and yourself? If yes, describe your experiences. If no, are you more open to such a connection, having read through this book?
2. Have you ever stood barefoot on the ground and felt the energy coming up through your feet into your body? Or the energy coming down from the sky into your head and down into your body?
3. Reflect on a time when you felt completely in sync with the people and events going on around you. Describe what it felt like. Next, reflect on a time when you felt out of sync, and describe what that was like.
4. Look at the "Dimensions" Table in Appendix B. Have you had experiences in each of these Dimensions? Give examples.
5. What does "ascension" mean to you?

Practice

1. Look up the phrase, "As above, so below." How does it relate to the information presented in this chapter, and the Appendices?
2. Research the etymologies of dimension, density, chakra, ascension, aura, astral, and any other terms used in this chapter that are related to your place in the universe. What do you find? Does this expand your understanding of how your personal existence coordinates with the whole universe?
3. Randomly select any chapter from the book (except for Chapters 1 or 32) and read it while paying special attention

to how it relates to this Coordinate chapter. How does the chapter you selected:

- Use all of your major chakras in a balanced way?
- Help you vibrate at higher frequencies?
- Help you feel connected to all that exists around you?
- Contribute to your ascension into higher Dimensions?

4. Repeat Practice #3 for the remaining chapters. (This will take a lot of time, but you've got the rest of your life.)

5. Remembering the computer analogy from the Preface: consider that Chapters 2–32 are functions and applications (apps) that, when put into practice, make you fully human.

- Which functions and apps are your favorite, and why?
- Which functions and apps are the easiest for you to practice, and which ones are more difficult?
- What functions and apps would you add to the 31 addressed in this book? In other words, what verbs would you add, and why?

6. Revisit the etymologies of the book title's words in Chapter 1.

- Do you find deeper meaning in these descriptions, now that you've read the whole book? Explain.
- Have the ancient practices recommended throughout the book prepared you well for reviving your indigenous soul? For participating in the ascension that this new age offers us? Why or why not?

7. Celebrate your successful practices.

8. Repeat as needed.

APPENDIX A
MAYA COORDINATES

Maya Coordinates

Reference: *The Energies of the Day: The Predictions of the Sacred Maya Calendar for 2012* by Denise Barrios & Denise De Peña; La Antigua, Guatemala: Mystic Maya Publications, 2012.

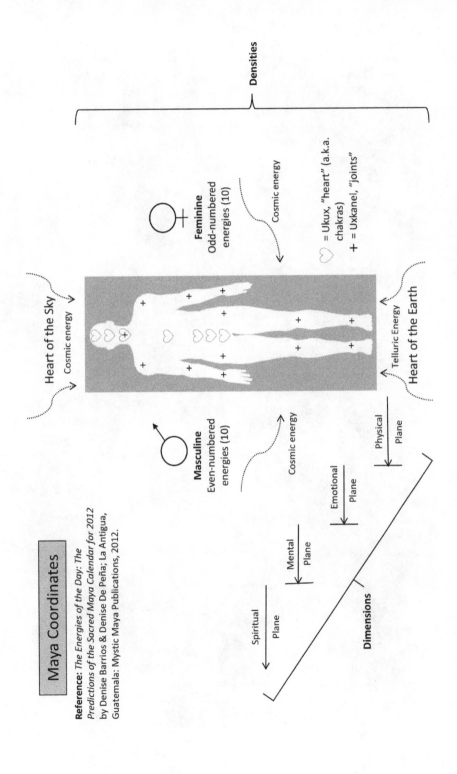

Densities

Feminine
Odd-numbered energies (10)

Cosmic energy

♡ = Ukux, "heart" (a.k.a. chakras)
+ = Uxkanel, "joints"

Heart of the Sky
Cosmic energy

Heart of the Earth
Telluric Energy

Masculine
Even-numbered energies (10)

Cosmic energy

Physical Plane

Emotional Plane

Mental Plane

Spiritual Plane

Dimensions

APPENDIX B

DIMENSIONS

Comparison of 3rd, 4th, and 5th Dimensions

Feature/Dimension	3rd	4th*	5th
Plane	Physical, material. Matter over Mind.	Astral, Magical. Matter and Mind.	Etheric, Light, Heaven. New Earth/New Human. Mind over Matter.
Dichotomy	Polarity. Opposites/dualism (e.g., good/bad, love/hate, masculine/feminine).	Polarized realm of Light and Dark forms. Battle of good and evil forces here. Shifting from dualism to paradox.	Oneness; unity. Integration of opposite forces into neutral balance.
Time	Linear. Sequence of past, present, and future.	More present focused. Past becomes history, not path (shedding of attachments to the past, dropping victimhood). Future is what one makes happen with his/her thoughts.	Past, present, and future combined into the NOW. Time is not linear, but event-based: manifestations are driven by preceding events, not timelines.
Charge	Negative thoughts dominate, attracting negative manifestations.	Positive and negative in antagonistic relationship, requiring discernment: "Which do I feed?"	Yin/Yang relationship of positive and negative
Energy	Dense, heavy. Low (slow) vibration.	Less dense, lighter than 3rd dimension. Higher (faster) vibration.	Light (no density or heaviness). High (fast) vibration.
Experience/ Perception of Reality	Reliance on 5 senses to determine what is real. Instinct rather than intuition.	Intuition increases. "6th sense" awakens.	Spontaneous revelation. Intuition replaces 5 senses for information gathering.

*Temporary; now used as merely a springboard for Earth to ascend into 5th dimension; then will no longer exist

Feature/Dimension	3rd	4th	5th
Relationship	Illusion of separation from the spirit (i.e., only experience the secular/profane). Illusion of separation from others. Judgment.	Awakening to spirit realm and connection with it. Secular and spirit realms co-exist. Shifting from judgment to compassion.	Spiritual realm. No judgment; only compassion. No separation. Discretion on where to place and not place one's energy.
Social Emphasis	Conformity	Individuality	Unity *and* Diversity
Law	Human law – what is valid is whatever falls within human law and policy (scientific method, empirical evidence).	Shifting from Human Law to Cosmic/Divine Law.	Complete honoring of Cosmic/Divine Law.
Creation of Reality (Power)	Little self-power perceived. Events in one's life and environment come from external forces. Inclined to seek power or control over external environment.	Awakening to one's own power. Discovery of self as co-creator with divine forces. Experiences cooperation between externally-based power and power within.	Realization of power within to shape one's external environment. Manifestation of things from one's own thought. Creating with light patterns and frequencies.
Human Doing	React	Respond	Create
Motivation	Fear. Love is conditional.	Trust. Working out karma from past lives.	Unconditional love.
Free Will	At conscious level, the illusion of no choice. Unconscious beliefs and external conditions direct reactions.	Awakening to possibility of choice.	Choice based on higher consciousness. Complete understanding and utilization of free will in a "do no harm" way.
Mortality/Finitude	Sees self as mortal/finite.	Sees possibility of immortality.	Immortality and infinity are realized.

APPENDIX C

CHAKRAS, SUBTLE BODIES, AND AURAS

Chakras, Subtle Bodies, and Auras

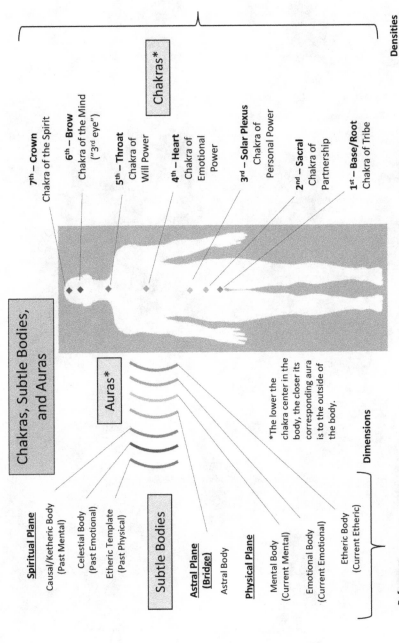

Chakras*

7th – Crown
Chakra of the Spirit

6th – Brow
Chakra of the Mind
("3rd eye")

5th – Throat
Chakra of
Will Power

4th – Heart
Chakra of
Emotional
Power

3rd – Solar Plexus
Chakra of
Personal Power

2nd – Sacral
Chakra of
Partnership

1st – Base/Root
Chakra of Tribe

Densities

Auras*

*The lower the
chakra center in the
body, the closer its
corresponding aura
is to the outside of
the body.

Dimensions

Subtle Bodies

Spiritual Plane
Causal/Ketheric Body
(Past Mental)

Celestial Body
(Past Emotional)

Etheric Template
(Past Physical)

**Astral Plane
(Bridge)**
Astral Body

Physical Plane
Mental Body
(Current Mental)

Emotional Body
(Current Emotional)

Etheric Body
(Current Etheric)

References:
1) *Anatomy of the Spirit: The Seven Stages of Power and Healing* by Carolyn Myss. Three Rivers Press, NY: 1996
2) "Guide to Self Healing," 2nd. Ed. (2000). http://www.gentletouchhealing.org.uk/forms/GTH GUIDE.pdf
3) "Energetic Anatomy: A Complete Guide to the Human Energy Fields and Etheric Bodies," by Cyndi Dale.
   http://www.gentletouchhealing.org.uk/forms/GTH GUIDE.pdf

APPENDIX D
ASCENSION TRAJECTORY

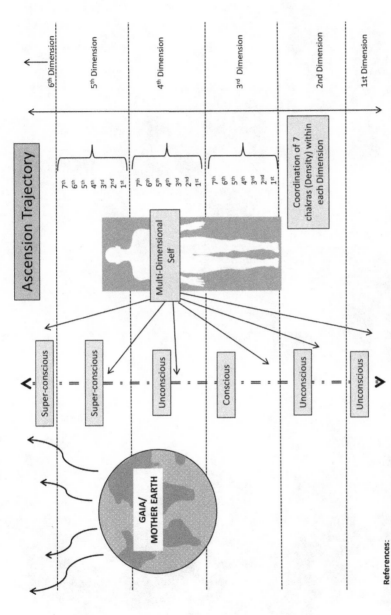

Ascension Trajectory

Multi-Dimensional Self

Coordination of 7 chakras (Density) within each Dimension

6th Dimension
5th Dimension
4th Dimension
3rd Dimension
2nd Dimension
1st Dimension

Super-conscious
Super-conscious
Unconscious
Conscious
Unconscious
Unconscious

GAIA/ MOTHER EARTH

References:
1) "Dimensions and Densities . . . According to the Channeled Sources" by Wes Penre, Feb. 1, 2012.
www.bibliotecapleyades.net/ciencia/ciencia_dimenstionshyperdimensions22.htm.
2) "What is Multidimensional Consciousness" by Suzan Caroll, January 2011. www.bibliotecapleyades.net/ciencia/ciencia_consciousuniverse121.htm

REFERENCES

Aleph, Faena. "Wopida: A Dakota Ceremony of Universal Gratitude," *Faena Aleph,* January 24, 2017, http://www.faena.com/aleph/articles/wopida-a-dakota-ceremony-of-universal-gratitude/.

Ashley. "The Third, Fourth, and Fifth Dimensions." *The Awakened State.* http://theawakenedstate.tumblr.com/post/35314404728/the-third-fourth-and-fifth-dimensions.

Backman, Linda. "Ego Versus Soul, Love, and Humility: Moving to 2012 and Beyond." In *2012: Creating Your Own Shift,* edited by Adonna and Hunt Henion, 101-104. USA: Shift Awareness Books, 2011.

Barrios, Carlos. *The Book of Destiny: Unlocking the Secrets of the Ancient Mayans and the Prophecy of 2012.* New York: Harper One, 2009.

Barrios, Denise, and Denise De Peña. *The Energies of the Day: The Predictions of the Sacred Maya Calendar for 2012.* La Antigua, Guatemala: Mystic Maya Publications, 2012.

Benson, Robert. *Between the Dreaming and the Coming True: The Road Home to God.* New York: Tarcher/Putnam, 2001.

Bryden, Joseph. *The Orenda.* New York, NY: Vintage Books, 2013.

Caroll, Suzan. "What is Multidimensional Consciousness?" *Biblioteca Pleyades*, January 2011, http://www.bibliotecapleyades.net/ciencia/ciencia_consciousuniverse121.htm.

Castaneda, Carlos. *The Teachings of Don Juan: A Yaqui Way of Knowledge*. New York, NY: Washington Square Press, 1974.

Christi, Nicolya. *2012 – A Clarion Call: Your Soul's Purpose in Conscious Evolution*. Rochester VT: Bear and Company, 2011.

Christi, Nicolya. *Contemporary Spirituality for an Evolving World: A Handbook for Conscious Evolution*. Rochester VT: Bear and Company, 2013.

Christi, Nicolya. *New Human – New Earth: Living in the 5th Dimension* (2012). EBook.

Da Jesus Book: Hawaii Pidgin New Testament. Orlando FL: Wycliffe Bible Translators, 2000.

Dale, Cyndi. "Energetic Anatomy: A Complete Guide to the Human Energy Fields and Etheric Bodies." *Conscious Lifestyle Magazine*. http://www.gentletouchhealing.org.uk/forms/GTH_GUIDE.pdf.

"Dimensions of Consciousness." *Peace in Practice*. February 2007. http://www.peaceinpractice.iinet.net.au/dimensionsofconsciousness.htm.

Douglas-Klotz, Neil. *Prayers of the Cosmos: Meditations on the Aramaic Words of Jesus*. San Francisco: Harper San Francisco, 1990.

Eastman, Charles Alexander (Ohi'ye S'a). *The Soul of the Indian: An Interpretation*. Boston, MA: Houghton Mifflin Co., 1911.

Eisenstein, Charles. *Sacred Economics: Money, Gift & Society in the Age of Transition*. Berkeley, CA: Evolver Editions, 2011.

Enerchi. "Structure of the Universe." *Ascension with Mother Earth and Current State of Affairs*. http://www.ascensionwithearth.com/p/structure-of-universe.html.

Estes, Clarissa Pinkola. *The Radiant Coat: Myths & Stories About the Crossing Between Life & Death*. CDs. Sounds True. 1991.

Findlow, Bruce, and Patrick L. Rickey. "For All That Is Our Life." In *Singing the Living Tradition*, 128. Boston, MA: Beacon Press/ Unitarian Universalist Association, 1993.

Fox, Matthew. *Original Blessing: A Primer in Creation Spirituality*. Santa Fe, NM: Bear & Company Publishing, 1983.

G, Akemi. *Why We Are Born: Remembering Our Purpose Through the Akashic Records*. CreateSpace Independent Publishing Platform, 2014. Ebook.

Garrett, J.T., and Michael Garrett. *Medicine of the Cherokee: The Way of Right Relationship*. Rochester, VT: Bear and Company, 1996.

Harper, Douglas. "Online Etymology Dictionary," www.etymonline.com.

Healer Members of Gentle Touch Healing. *Guide to Self Healing*, 2*nd* ed. England: Gentle Touch Healing, LTD, 2000. http://www. gentletouchhealing.org.uk/forms/GTH_GUIDE.pdf.

Jenkinson, Stephen. *Angel or Executioner: Grief and the Love of Life*. 4-CD set. Canada: Orphan Wisdom, 2009.

Jenkinson, Stephen. *Die Wise: A Manifesto for Sanity and Soul*. Berkeley, CA: North Atlantic Books, 2015.

Jenkinson, Stephen. *Money and the Soul's Desires: A Meditation*. 5-CD set. Canada: OrphanWisdom, 2002.

Jensen, Derrick. "Saving the Indigenous Soul: An Interview with Martin Prechtel." *The Sun Magazine,* no. 304 (2001). Accessed June 13, 2013. http://www.hiddenwine.com/indexSUN.html).

Kohlenberger III, John R., Edward W. Goodrick, and James A. Swanson. *The Greek English Concordance to the New Testament With the New International Version.* Grand Rapids, MI: Zondervan Publishing House, 1997.

Lawlor, Robert. *Voices of the First Day: Awakening in the Aboriginal Dreamtime.* Rochester, VT: Inner Traditions International, LTD., 1991.

Lie, Sue. "Your Intimate Relationship with Gaia's Ascension – The Arcturians." *Sananda Website.* January 11, 2016. http://sananda.website/the-arkturians-via-suzanne-lie-jauary-11ᵗʰ.

Life Prayers From Around the World: 365 Prayers, Blessings, and Affirmations to Celebrate the Human Journey, Edited by Elizabeth Roberts and Elias Amidon. San Francisco: HarperSanFrancisco, 1996.

Macdonald, Helen. *H is for Hawk.* New York, NY: Grove Press, 2014.

McCarty, James Allen, Don Elkins, and Carla Rueckert. "The Law of One: Book II." *L/L Research.* 1982.

Myss, Caroline. *Anatomy of the Spirit: The Seven Stages of Power and Healing.* New York: Three Rivers Press, 1996.

Myss, Caroline. *Sacred Contracts: Awakening Your Divine Potential.* New York: Harmony Books, 2001.

Newton, Dawn. "The 2012 Phenomena: The Transformation of Humanity and Their Planet." In *2012: Creating Your Own Shift,* edited by Adonna and Hunt Henion, 31-33. USA: Shift Awareness Books, 2011.

Nuno. "Densities Chart." *Heartki*. July 15, 2016. http://www.heartki. com/densities-chart/.

O'Donohue, John. *To Bless the Space Between Us: A Book of Blessings.* New York, NY: Doubleday, 2008.

Penre, Wes. "Dimensions and Densities . . . According to the Channeled Sources." *Biblioteca Pleyades.* February 1, 2013. http://www.bibliotecapleyades.net/ciencia/ciencia_dimension shyperdimensions22.htm.

Prechtel, Martin. *Long Life, Honey in the Heart: A Story of Initiation and Eloquence from the Shores of a Mayan Lake.* Berkeley, CA: North Atlantic Books, 1999.

Prechtel, Martin. *Secrets of the Talking Jaguar: Memoirs from the Living Heart of a Mayan Village.* New York: Tarcher/Putnam, 1999.

Prechtel, Martin. *Stealing Benefacio's Roses.* Berkeley, CA: North Atlantic Books, 2002.

Prechtel, Martin. *The Disobedience of the Daughter of the Sun: A Mayan Tale of Ecstasy, Time, and Finding One's True Form.* Berkeley, CA: North Atlantic Books, 2001.

Prechtel, Martin. *The Unlikely Peace at Cuchumaquic – The Parallel Lives of People as Plants: Keeping the Seeds Alive.* Berkeley, CA: North Atlantic Books, 2012.

"Proto-Indo-Europeans," Wikipedia Foundation, Inc. Last modified March 6, 2017. https://en.wikipedia.org/wiki/Proto-Indo-Europeans.

Rachele, Sal. "Dimensions and Densities. *Living Awareness Productions,* 2016. http://www.salrachele.com/webarticles/dimensionsand densities.htm.

Rael, Joseph. *Sound: Native Teachings + Visionary Art*. San Francisco: Council Art Books, 2009.

Sams, Jamie. *Dancing the Dream: The Seven Sacred Paths of Human Transformation*. San Francisco:HarperSanFrancisco, 1998.

Sams, Jamie. *Earth Medicine: Ancestors' Ways of Harmony for Many Moons*. New York, NY: HarperCollins, 1994.

Sams, Jamie. *Sacred Path Cards: The Discovery of Self Through Native Teachings*. New York, NY: Harper Collins, 1990.

Sams, Jamie and David Carson. *Medicine Cards: The Discovery of Power Through the Ways of Animals*. New York, NY: St. Martin's Press, 1999.

Sams, Jamie and Twylah Nitsch. *Other Council Fires Were Here Before Ours*. San Francisco: Harper San Francisco, 1991.

Sapp, Nikkij. "3rd, 4th, & 5th Dimension Reality Overview." *Secret Energy*. http://secretenergy.com/news/3rd-4th-5th-dimension-reality-overview/.

Self, Jim. "What Do You Mean the 3rd Dimension is Going Away?" *in5d: Esoteric Metaphysical Spiritual Data Base*. March 6, 2015. http://in5d.com/what-do-you-mean-the-3rd-dimension-is-going-away/.

Shimer, Porter. *Healing Secrets of the Native Americans*. New York, NY: Tess Press, 2004.

Some´, Malidoma Patrice. *Of Water and the Spirit: Ritual, Magic, and Initiation in the Life of an African Shaman*. NY: Penguin Group, 1994.

Some´, Malidoma Patrice. *Ritual: Power, Healing, and Community*. New York: Penguin Compass, 1993.

Some´, Malidoma Patrice. *The Healing Wisdom of Africa: Finding Life Purpose Through Nature, Ritual, and Community*. New York: Penguin Putnam, 1998.

Sproul, Barbara C. *Primal Myths: Creation Myths Around the World*. New York: HarperOne, 1979.

Steinbeck, John. *The Grapes of Wrath*. New York, NY: Viking Press, 1989.

Tyndall, Rona. "Becoming and Belonging." *Quest* 71, no. 9 (2016): 1-2.

The HarperCollins Study Bible: New Revised Standard Version, edited by Wayne E. Meeks, Jouette M. Bassler, Werner E. Lemke, Susan Niditch, and Eileen M. Schuller. New York NY: HarperCollins Publishers, 1993.

The Wisdom of the Native Americans, edited by Kent Nerburn. Novato CA: New World Library, 1999.

Wells, Barbara, and Jaco B. Ten Hove. *Articulating Your UU Faith*. Boston, MA: Beacon Press/Unitarian Universalist Association, 2003.

Wilkinson, Justin. "An Introduction to Change." In *2012: Creating Your Own Shift*, edited by Adonna and Hunt Henion, 27-29. USA: Shift Awareness Books, 2011.

Young, Jon. *What the Robin Knows: How Birds Reveal the Secrets of the Natural World*. New York: Houghton Mifflin, 2012.

ENDNOTES

1   Douglas Harper, "Online Etymology Dictionary," www.etymonline.com.
2   "Proto-Indo-Europeans," Wikipedia Foundation, Inc., last modified March 6, 2017, https://en.wikipedia.org/wiki/Proto-Indo-Europeans.
3   Martin Prechtel, *The Unlikely Peace at Cuchumaquic – The Parallel Lives of People as Plants: Keeping the Seeds Alive* (Berkeley, CA: North Atlantic Books, 2012), 433–434.
4   Joseph Rael, *Sound: Native Teachings + Visionary Art* (San Francisco: Council Art Books, 2009), 59.
5   Linda Backman, "Ego Versus Soul, Love, and Humility: Moving to 2012 and Beyond," in *2012: Creating Your Own Shift*, eds. Adonna and Hunt Henion (USA: Shift Awareness Books, 2011), 101.
6   Carlos Barrios, *The Book of Destiny: Unlocking the Secrets of the Ancient Mayans and the Prophecy of 2012* (New York, NY: HarperOne, 2009), 119.
7   Barrios, *op. cit.*, 121.
8   Barrios, *op. cit.*, 123.
9   Barrios, *op. cit.*, 124.
10 Jamie Sams, *Earth Medicine: Ancestors' Ways of Harmony for Many Moons* (New York, NY: HarperCollins, 1994), 65.
11 Martin Prechtel, *Long Life, Honey in the Heart: A Story of Initiation and Eloquence from the Shores of a Mayan Lake* (Berkeley, CA: North Atlantic Books, 1999), 5.
12 Prechtel, *op. cit.*, 349.
13 *Ibid.*
14 Stephen Jenkinson, *Money and the Soul's Desires: A Meditation*, CD set (Canada: Orphan Wisdom, 2002).
15 Charles Eisenstein, *Sacred Economics: Money, Gift and Society in the Age of Transition* (Berkeley, CA: Evolver Editions, 2011), 344.
16 Barrios, *op. cit.*, 128.
17 Rona Tyndall, "Becoming and Belonging," *Quest*, October 2016, 1.
18 Rael, *op. cit.*, 48, 71.
19 Rael, *op. cit.*, 40, 177.

20   Barrios, *op.cit.*, 124.

21   Rael, *op. cit.*, 144.

22   James Allen McCarty, Don Elkins, and Carla Rueckert, "The Law of One: Book II," *L/L Research*, 1982, www.llresearch.org/library/the_law_of_one_pdf/the_law_of_one_book_2.pdf.

23   Nicolya Christi, *New Human - New Earth: Living in the 5th Dimension* (2012). EBook, 30.

24   Barrios, *op cit.*, 164, 167.

25   Myss, Caroline, *Sacred Contracts: Awakening Your Divine Potential* (New York: Harmony Books, 2001).

26   Jamie Sams, *Sacred Path Cards: The Discovery of Self Through Native Teachings* (New York: Harper Collins, 1990).

27   Jamie Sams and David Carson, *Medicine Cards: The Discovery of Power Through the Ways of Animals* (New York: St. Martin's Press, 1999).

28   Robert Lawlor, *Voices of the Day* (Rochester, VT: Inner Traditions International, 1991), 48–49

29   Derrick Jensen, "Saving the Indigenous Soul: An Interview with Martin Prechtel," *The Sun*, no. 304 (2001). Accessed in June 13, 2013, http://www.hiddenwine.com/indexSUN.html.

30   Martin Prechtel, *Secrets of the Talking Jaguar: Memoirs From the Living Heart of a Mayan Village* (New York: Tarcher/Putnam, 1999), 170.

31   Joseph Rael, *op.cit.*, 118.

32   James Allen McCarty, Don Elkins, and Carla Rueckert, *op cit.*, 88, 89.

33   Jamie Sams and Twylah Nitsch, *Other Council Fires Were Here Before Ours* (San Francisco: Harper San Francisco, 1991), 121.

34   Martin Prechtel, *The Unlikely Peace at Cuchumaquic – The Parallel Lives of People as Plants: Keeping the Seeds Alive* (Berkeley, CA: North Atlantic Books, 2012), 329.

35   *Ibid.*

36   Jon Young, *What the Robin Knows: How Birds Reveal the Secrets of the Natural World* (New York: Houghton Mifflin, 2012), xxv.

37   Jamie Sams and Twylah Nitsch, *op. cit.,* 70.

38   Malidoma Some´, *The Healing Wisdom of Africa: Finding Life Purpose Through Nature, Ritual, and Community* (New York: Penguin Putnam, 1998), 52.

39   Jamie Sams and Twylah Nitsch, *op. cit.,* 49.

40   Martin Prechtel, *Long Life, Honey in the Heart: A Story of Initiation and Eloquence from the Shores of a Mayan Lake* (Berkeley, CA: North Atlantic Books, 1999), 56.

41   Joseph Rael, *op. cit.*, 165.

42   Neil Douglas-Klotz, *Prayers of the Cosmos: Meditations on the Aramaic Words of Jesus* (San Francisco: Harper San Francisco, 1990), 31.

43   Malidoma Some´, *op. cit.*, 78.

44   Martin Prechtel, *The Unlikely Peace at Cuchumaquic – The Parallel Lives of People as Plants: Keeping the Seeds Alive* (Berkeley, CA: North Atlantic Books, 2012), 313.

45   John Kohlenberger, Edward Goodrick, and James Swanson, *The Greek English Concordance to the New Testament with the New International Version* (Grand Rapids, MI: Zondervan Publishing House, 1997), 328.

46   *Ibid*, 636.

47   Carlos Castaneda, *The Teachings of Don Juan: A Yaqui Way of Knowledge* (New York, NY: Washington Square Press, 1974), 107.

48   Joseph Bryden, *The Orenda* (New York, NY: Vintage Books, 2012), 78-79.

49   Jamie Sams, *Earth Medicine: Ancestors' Ways of Harmony for Many Moons* (New York, NY: Harper Collins, 1990), 124.

50   Martin Prechtel, *Secrets of the Talking Jaguar: Memoirs From the Living Heart of a Mayan Village* (New York: Tarcher/Putnam, 1999), 116, 117.

51   Barbara Wells and Jaco B. Ten Hove, *Articulating Your UU Faith* (Boston, MA: Beacon Press/Unitarian Universalist Association, 2003).

52   Martin Prechtel, *The Disobedience of the Daughter of the Sun: A Mayan Tale of Ecstasy, Time, and Finding One's True Form* (Berkeley, CA: North Atlantic Books, 2001), 4-5.

53   Barbara Sproul, *Primal Myths: Creation Myths Around the World* (New York: HarperOne, 1979), 2.

54   Martin Prechtel, *The Disobedience of the Daughter of the Sun: A Mayan Tale of Ecstasy, Time, and Finding One's True Form* (Berkeley, CA: North Atlantic Books, 2001), 87.

55   Matthew Fox, *Original Blessing: A Primer in Creation Spirituality* (Santa Fe, NM: Bear & Company, 1983).

56   John O'Donohue, *To Bless the Space Between Us: A Book of Blessings* (New York, NY: Doubleday, 2008), 198.

57   *Ibid.*, 9.

58   Malidoma Some´, *Ritual: Power, Healing, and Community* (New York, NY: Penguin Compass, 1993), 15-17, 59.

59   Akemi G, *Why We Are Born: Remembering Our Purpose Through the Akashic Records* (CreateSpace Independent Publishing Platform, 2014) Ebook, 124.

60   Charles Alexander Eastman (Ohi'ye S'a), *The Soul of the Indian: An Interpretation* (Boston, MA: Houghton Mifflin, 1911), 45-46.

61   Faena Aleph, "Wopida: A Dakota Ceremony of Universal Gratitude," *Faena Aleph,* January 24, 2017, http://www.faena.com/aleph/articles/wopida-a-dakota-ceremony-of-universal-gratitude/.

62   Jamie Sams, *Earth Medicine: Ancestors' Ways of Harmony for Many Moons* (New York, NY: Harper Collins, 1990), 240.

63   Robert Benson, *Between the Dreaming and the Coming True: The Road Home to God* (New York: Tarcher/Putnam, 2001), 135.

64   Malidoma Some´, *The Healing Wisdom of Africa: Finding Life Purpose Through Nature, Ritual, and Community* (New York: Penguin Putnam, 1998), 143, 146.

65   Bruce Findlow, "For All That is Our Life," In *Singing the Living Tradition* (Boston, MA: Beacon Press/Unitarian Universalist Association, 1993), 128.

66   Malidoma Some´, *op. cit.*, 123.

67   Stephen Jenkinson, *Angel or Executioner: Grief and the Love of Life*, CD set. (Canada: Orphan Wisdom, 2009).

68   Stephen Jenkinson, *Die Wise: A Manifesto for Sanity and Soul* (Berkeley, CA: North Atlantic Books, 2015).

69   Clarissa Pinkola Estes, *The Radiant Coat: Myths & Stories About the Crossing Between Life & Death*, CDs, Sounds True, 1991.

70   Jamie Sams, *op.cit.*, 361.

71   Denise Barrios and Denise De Peña. *The Energies of the Day: The Predictions of the Sacred Maya Calendar for 2012* (La Antigua, Guatemala: Mystic Maya Publications, 2012), 3.

72   Suzan Caroll, "What is Multidimensional Consciousness?" *Biblioteca Pleyades*, January 2011, http://www.bibliotecapleyades.net/ciencia/ciencia_consciousuniverse121.htm.

73   Sal Rachele, "Dimensions and Densities," *Living Awareness Productions,* 2016, http://www.salrachele.com/webarticles/dimensionsanddensities.htm.

74   Caroline Myss, *Anatomy of the Spirit: The Seven Stages of Power and Healing.* (New York, NY: Three Rivers Press, 1996), 68-70, 79.

75   Suzan Caroll, *op. cit.*, 1.